THE TIMOTHY INITIATIVE

New Testament Gospels

Greg Kappas and Jared Nelms, EDS.

New Testament Gospels
Book Six in TTI's Foundational Curriculum

© 2012 by The Timothy Initiative

International Standard Book Number: 978-1477582800

All rights reserved. Published and Printed in the United States of America.

Library of Congress Cataloging-in-Publication Data

No part of this book covered by the copyrights heron may be reproduced or copied
in any form or by any means without written permission of the publisher.

Scripture quotations are from: The New King James Version
Copyright © 1979, 1980, 1982 by Thomas Nelson, Inc.
Used by permission. All rights reserved.

First Edition-North America
Second Edition

Acknowledgements

TTI gives special gratitude to the Docent Group and the leadership of Glenn Lucke and Jared Wilson (Docent Executive Editor for this project). The Docent writer, Eric Stanford has demonstrated outstanding insight and followed the project requests extremely well. We are also very grateful for Pastor Jesse Nelms and his diligent, discerning edit of this manuscript.

TTI also gives thanks to Dr. David Nelms, our Founder/President for his vision and influence to see this New Curriculum written. Dr. Nelms has lived humbly to see you succeed greatly in Jesus Christ.

We express our gratitude for the fine, long editorial labor to TTI Executive Editor and Director, Dr. Greg Kappas and the Executive Editorial Assistant and International Director, Rev. Jared Nelms. In addition we thank the entire TTI editorial team of Dr. David Nelms, Rev. Jesse Nelms, Rev. Larry Starkey, Rev. Lou Mancari and Dr. David Nichols. Each of you has given such remarkable grace to us and now to these church planters. TTI is greatly appreciative of the Grace Fellowship elders, pastors, administrative staff, leaders and GF family. TTI was birthed out of this "church for all nations." Thank you for your generosity in launching this exponential network of church planting movements.

TTI's Board of Directors has given us freedom and focus to excel still more. We are deeply moved by these men and women of God. Our TTI investor base of financial and prayer partners extend around the globe. These individuals, churches, ministries, networks, corporations and organizations are essential and strategic to our collective health and Kingdom impact. Thank you!

We thank the TTI Continental Directors, Regional Directors, National Directors and District/Training Center Leaders for your ministry of love and commitment. You are the ones that forge into new and current frontiers with the Gospel. You truly are our heroes.

Finally, we are forever grateful to you, the church planter. You are planting an orchard, a church planting center through your local church that will touch your region and the world with the Gospel of Jesus Christ. We are honored to serve the Lord Jesus Christ and you. You will make a difference for our great God as you multiply healthy churches for His glory. We love you and believe in you!

The Timothy Initiative Staff Team
September 2010

THE TIMOTHY INITIATIVE

"What you have heard from me in the presence of many witnesses entrust to faithful men who will be able to teach others also."

2 Timothy 2:2

This workbook is the sixth of 10 workbooks which assist in equipping church planting leaders to start churches that saturate a region and help reach every man, woman and child with the Good News of our Lord. Below is the list of this initial Curriculum.

TTI Curriculum

Workbook Number/Course:

1. Hermeneutics

2. Homiletics

3. Church Planting (New Testament – Acts, Evangelism, Discipleship, Spiritual Life, T4T)

4. Old Testament 1

5. Old Testament 2

6. **New Testament Gospels**

7. New Testament Pastoral Epistles

8. New Testament General Letters

9. Major Bible Doctrines

10. Apologetics-Church History-Spiritual Warfare

TABLE OF CONTENTS

Part 1: The Four Gospels

Chapter 1: An Introduction to the Gospels 10

Chapter 2: A Fourfold Portrayal of Jesus 14

Chapter 3: Tough Questions about the Gospels 18

Chapter 4: An Overview & Outline of Matthew 22

Chapter 5: An Overview & Outline of Mark 30

Chapter 6: An Overview & Outline of Luke 36

Chapter 7: An Overview & Outline of John 42

Chapter 8: The Words of Jesus 50

Part 2: The Life and Ministry of Jesus

Chapter 9: An Introduction to the Life of Jesus 56

Chapter 10: The Messiah's Preparations 66

Chapter 11: The Beginning of the Work 72

Chapter 12: A Time of Popularity 76

Chapter 13: A Time of Rejection 86

Chapter 14: Heading Toward the Cross 92

Chapter 15: The Work of Redemption Begun 102

Chapter 16: The Work of Redemption Completed 110

Appendix: Outline for Studying the Life of Christ 118

Endnotes 126

Additional Resource Guide 128

Part 1: The Four Gospels

Chapter One
An Introduction to the Gospels

The Gospels are the first four books of the New Testament, called Matthew, Mark, Luke, and John after the names of the men who wrote them. The name "Gospel" comes from a Greek word that means "good news." The first time that word appears is in *Mark 1:1: "The beginning of the gospel of Jesus Christ, the Son of God."*

The first three Gospels-Matthew, Mark, and Luke-were probably all written about twenty or thirty years after Jesus' death. John was probably written about fifty or sixty years after Jesus' death. The authors all either knew Jesus personally or were closely connected with people who knew Jesus.

The four Gospels agree with each other in that they all show us the same Jesus and teach a gospel of salvation.

The Purpose of the Gospels

Although all of the Gospels focus on the life of Jesus, they are not biographies like the biographies we might read about famous people today. None of the Gospels gives a detailed account of Jesus' life straight through from birth to death, though some (such as Luke), give more details of His life than others do. Instead, they note key events and teachings that together describe the good news that God saves us from our sins through Christ. It is not surprising, then, that each of the Gospels focuses most heavily on the events leading up to the death and resurrection of Jesus.

The Gospels are history with a purpose. Their intention is to help people believe in Jesus. As the Gospel of John says near its conclusion, *"And truly Jesus did many other signs in the presence of His disciples, which are not written in this book; but these are written that you may believe that Jesus is the Christ, the Son of God, and that believing you may have life in His name"* (*John 20:30-31*).

With the Gospels, God's promise of life comes to the forefront. Written for both Jews and Gentiles, they show us the Messiah whose death brings us eternal life through a gift of grace to all who believe in Him. Christians and non-Christians alike should seek to become familiar with the Gospels and therefore with the Savior those Gospels portray.

The Four Gospels

As we shall see in more depth as we go along, each of the four Gospels has a particular people in mind and has a special way of looking at Jesus. They all instruct believers and introduce unbelievers to the Savior.

1. Matthew was written to Jews and presents Jesus as the King of the Jews.

2. Mark was written to Romans and focuses on Jesus as a Servant.

3. Luke was written to Greeks and shows Jesus as the Son of Man.

4. John was written to both Jews and Gentiles, to all people, and shows Jesus as the Son of God.

Traditionally, the four Gospels have been symbolized by the four creatures mentioned in *Ezekiel 1:5-11* and *Revelation 4:6-7*.

1. Lion → Matthew: This symbol of royalty fits the King of the Jews.

2. Ox → Mark: The ox was a symbol of servanthood, appropriate for the Divine Servant.

3. Man → Luke: Jesus was a human like us.

4. Eagle → John: Jesus was Divine, as symbolized by the soaring eagle.[1]

Key Verses of the Gospels

One could choose any number of powerful verses to represent each of the Gospels. The following four reflect the special character of each of the four books.

1. The Gospel of Matthew—Jesus' kingship:
   "And they put up over His head the accusation written against Him: THIS IS JESUS THE KING OF THE JEWS" (Matthew 27:37).

2. The Gospel of Mark—Jesus' servanthood:
   "For even the Son of Man did not come to be served, but to serve, and to give His life a ransom for many" (Mark 10:45).

3. The Gospel of Luke—Jesus' humanity:
   "For the Son of Man has come to seek and to save that which was lost" (Luke 19:10).

4. The Gospel of John—Jesus' divinity:
   "For God so loved the world that He gave His only begotten Son, that whoever believes in Him should not perish but have everlasting life" (John 3:16).

NOTES

The Gospels' Authors

1. <u>Matthew</u> (also known as Levi): A tax collector and disciple of Jesus (see *Mark 2:13-17*).

2. <u>Mark</u>: A missionary with Barnabas and Paul (see *Acts 12:12, 25; 13:5, 13; 15:36-39; Colossians 4:10; 2 Timothy 4:11; Philemon 1:24; 1 Peter 5:13*).

3. <u>Luke</u>: A Greek doctor who traveled with Paul. Luke also wrote Acts (*Colossians 4:14; 2 Timothy 4:11; Philemon 1:24*).

4. <u>John</u>: A fisherman, disciple of Jesus, and leader of the early church. Also wrote 1 John, 2 John, 3 John, and Revelation (see *Matthew 4:21-22; 17:1; Mark 10:35-45; Luke 8:51; 22:8; John 13:23; 19:26-27; 21:20-24; Galatians 2:9; Revelation 1:1*).

How the Gospels Were Created

Bible scholars call Matthew, Mark, and Luke the "Synoptic Gospels." The word "Synoptic" comes from a Greek term meaning "seeing together." These three books tend to see Jesus in much the same way. Simply put, they are similar. In many cases, their reports of certain events or teachings are exactly the same.

Probably the authors Matthew, Mark, and Luke used similar sources for their Gospels. We're not exactly sure how it worked. But certainly a group of stories and sayings of Jesus were being repeated within the church. Furthermore, some scholars think that the Gospel of Mark was written first and that Matthew and Luke in part based their own Gospels on Mark's Gospel.

The Gospel of John is more different from the others. It seems that John decided to write in a different way about the Jesus story. His own special purposes, and his own special writing style, helped to make this Gospel different from the others.

Why We Can Trust the Gospels

New Testament scholar Craig Blomberg explained why it matters whether we can believe the Gospels are true. He pointed out that the New Testament makes claims about Christianity being rooted in real historical events. So the accuracy of these claims is important. Blomberg went on to say, *"For Christianity, the central story is about the life, death, and resurrection of Jesus, the story that forms the topic of the four New Testament Gospels."*[2]

So, can we trust the Gospels? Yes, for at least three reasons.

1. **The Gospel writers were careful about the facts**

    "Inasmuch as many have taken in hand to set in order a narrative of those things which have been fulfilled among us, just as those who from the begin-

ning were eyewitnesses and ministers of the word delivered them to us, it seemed good to me also, having had perfect understanding of all things from the very first, to write to you an orderly account, most excellent Theophilus, that you may know the certainty of those things in which you were instructed" (Luke 1:1-4).

2. **The Holy Spirit ensured the accuracy of what the Gospel writers wrote**

   "The Helper, the Holy Spirit, whom the Father will send in My name, He will teach you all things, and bring to your remembrance all things that I said to you...He will guide you into all truth" (John 14:26; 16:13).

   "All Scripture is given by inspiration of God" (2 Timothy 3:16).

3. **The early church accepted and affirmed the Gospel accounts**

   The Gospels are not legends or myths. Instead, the Gospels are factual accounts written while many eyewitnesses were still living. If the accounts had been in error, people would have objected. But instead the leaders of the church accepted the Gospels, passed them around, and based their teachings about Jesus on them. As we will see in the chapters focused on the individual Gospels, early Christian "fathers" (leaders) such as Papias and Polycarp affirmed the authority of the Gospels.

Some of the questions we will consider include:

- Why did God give us four Gospels instead of just one?
- What should we think about places where the Gospels appear to disagree?
- How are the Gospels similar? How are they different?
- Do the words of Jesus have special value compared to the rest of the Bible?
- How can we come up with a time line of Jesus' life from the Gospels?
- What are the important events in Jesus' life that the Gospels teach us about?
- What are the important teachings of Jesus we should know about?
- What do the Gospels teach us about who Jesus is, who we are, and what God wants of us?

Questions

What is a Gospel?

What differences among the four Gospels are you beginning to see?

Why can we trust the Gospels? And why is that important to you and your ministry?

Chapter Two
A Fourfold Portrayal of Jesus

In his book *Four Portraits, One Jesus*, Mark Strauss tells about the time when a photographer was taking pictures of his two-year-old son. As little children will do, the boy quickly went through a range of emotions during the picture-taking session. Consequently, one picture shows the boy sitting quietly; another shows him laughing; another shows him getting bored; and still another shows him looking angry.

Which of these pictures captures his son's personality? The answer, of course, is all of them! Each one caught a different angle of his personality. Together they give an insightful view into who he is.[3]

It is the same for the Gospels. Each gives us a different glimpse of the same Savior.

Why Four Gospels?

Norman Geisler says there are at least three reasons why God decided to put four Gospels in the Bible.[4]

1. **To Establish the Truth**

    The Bible says, *"By the mouth of two or three witnesses every word may be established"* (*Matthew 18:16*; see *Deuteronomy 19:15*). With the Gospels, we have not just two or three but four witnesses to the truth about Jesus!

2. **To Better Reveal God's Glory**

    Speaking of Jesus, the Gospel of John says, *"The Word became flesh and dwelt among us, and we beheld His glory, the glory as of the only begotten of the Father, full of grace and truth"* (*John 1:14*). The four Gospels reveal different sides of the glory of God shown to us in Jesus.

3. **To Present Jesus to All People**

    As we have seen, Matthew was written to the Jews, Mark was written to the Romans, Luke was written to the Greeks, and John was written for the whole world. The Bible says, *"God so loved the world that He gave His only begotten Son, that whoever believes in Him should not perish but have everlasting life"* (*John 3:16*). It makes sense that God would want Gospels targeted to everyone in the world.

Other Gospels?

We might ask, why four Gospels? But we might also ask, why only four Gospels?

It is true that other Gospels were written. For example, there is a Gospel supposedly written by Peter and a Gospel supposedly written by Thomas.

All of these other Gospels were written long after Jesus and the apostles had died. None of them has the authority that the four New Testament Gospels have. <u>None of them are Scripture as Matthew, Mark, Luke, and John</u>.

Speaking of these other Gospels, Mark Strauss says, "While these writings might preserve an occasional authentic saying or story about Jesus, they are for the most part unreliable late compositions."[5]

We can be confident that Matthew, Mark, Luke, and John show the true picture of Jesus that God wanted the world to see.

Characteristics of the Biblical Gospels

Although the four Gospels of the New Testament have a lot in common, certain characteristics of the content and presentation in each Gospel stand out. See the tables below:[6]

The Gospel of Matthew:
Strong Jewish focus, with Jesus as the Jewish Messiah
Strong criticism of the Jewish religious leaders
Emphasis on the fulfillment of Hebrew prophecies
Interest in the Old Testament law
Emphasis on the kingdom
Five long sections of teaching material
Going back and forth between teaching and stories
Grouping of related material together
Messianic titles of Son of God, Christ, and Son of David
Emphasis on Jesus as the presence of God—"God with us"
Jesus portrayed as the new Israel and the new Moses
Jesus portrayed as Wisdom
Greater role for Peter than in the other Gospels
Emphasis on the mission to the Gentiles

NOTES

The Gospel of Mark:
Fast-moving story, with the frequent use of the idea of "immediately" and the present tense
Vivid descriptions of persons and events
Importance of Galilee as the location of Jesus' early ministry
Strong emphasis on Jesus' authority in teaching and in miracles
Emphasis on keeping quiet about Jesus' miracles and sayings
Amazed reaction by others to Jesus' authority
Emphasis on Jesus' defeat of challenges by Satan
Jesus as the Messiah, Son of God, and suffering Son of Man
Sinners are accepted through faith
The disciples poor model of how to follow Jesus
Long writing about the events surrounding Jesus' death
Short resurrection story

The Gospel of Luke:
Historical notes and dating related to Roman and Jewish leaders
Emphasis on the Gospel message being for all people
References to Jesus as Savior, Christ, Lord, and Prophet
Emphasis on promise and fulfillment
The presence of salvation in the words and deeds of Jesus
Jesus' concern for outsiders, such as the poor, sinners, and Samaritans
Emphasis on the reversal of fortunes, such as the rich becoming poor
Emphasis on women
The coming of the Holy Spirit as a sign of the new age
References to Jesus' prayer life and His teaching on prayer
References to praise, joy, and celebration because of God's salvation
The importance of Jerusalem and Jesus' journey there
Emphasis on the present reign of Christ

The Gospel of John:
Jesus as "the Word"
Emphasis on Jesus' identity as the Son who reveals the Father
Simple words with deep theological meaning
Key terms used: life, believe, abide, light
Key symbols used: water, light, bread, shepherd, gate
People presented as either "of God" or "of the world"

The Gospel of John continued:
Miracles identified as "signs" revealing Jesus' divine identity
"I am" statements by Jesus
People misunderstanding Jesus, especially His divine origin
Personal interviews with Jesus (Nicodemus, Samaritan woman)
Long teachings by Jesus
Debates between Jesus and religious leaders ("the Jews")
Use of Jewish festivals, especially Passover, to date the events
Clear statement of purpose: to call people to faith in Jesus
Teachings about the Holy Spirit as the Counselor Jesus gives us

The Same, Yet Different

On the one hand, we don't want to downplay too much what the four Gospels have in common. Each is about Jesus, and He is clearly the same in them all. As L. W. Hurtado says,

> *"Although there are numerous differences among them, the four Gospels exhibit a basically similar type of Jesus literature: (1) connected narratives of his ministry, death and resurrection; (2) compared out of the Jesus tradition; (3) reflecting and serving early Christian proclamation; (4) intended for Christian readers and presupposing their beliefs and vocabulary... They constitute a distinctive group of writings within early Christianity."*[7]

On the other hand, we shouldn't minimize the differences among the Gospels. The New Testament scholar Howard Marshall says, *"Each of the Gospel writers presents Jesus to us in his own characteristic way. The greatness of this person could not have been captured in one picture. So we have four portraits, each bringing out its own distinctive facets of the character of Jesus."*[8]

As the promise of life appears in Jesus, we see His beauty from different angles in the Four Gospels.

Questions

How are the Gospels the same?

How are the Gospels different?

Chapter Three
Questions about the Gospels

What a privilege it is to have the four Gospels to show us our Savior in different ways! We should become familiar with and treasure each one.

But this doesn't mean that we shouldn't be aware of some tough questions that some people may ask about the first four books of the New Testament and their portrayal of Jesus. The Gospels have withstood all tests for the past two thousand years. We have nothing to fear for them.

A Critical Approach to the Gospels

If you listen to some New Testament scholars speaking about the Gospels, you will realize that they do not believe that the Gospels were inspired by God and are reliable sources of information about Jesus. They will say that the Gospels preserve some true facts about Jesus and that they have some value for people who are interested in them. But these scholars don't hesitate to point out parts of the Gospel that they don't believe to be literally true.

The reason is that these Bible critics are anti-supernaturalists. That is, they don't believe that God does things in the world outside the usual operation of nature. So, when it comes to the Gospels, they deny the miracles of Jesus, deny prophecy (such as His prediction that the temple would be destroyed, which happened after His death), and deny His bodily resurrection. They think the Gospels were written long after the death of Jesus by people who may not have even known Him. In their view, the Gospels are filled with errors and made-up material.

Many of these kinds of critics are intelligent, well-educated people, and they can sound persuasive. But for two thousand years, God has used the Gospels to change lives by introducing people to the God-man Jesus, who really did the things that the Gospels say He did and who really said the things the Gospels say He did. <u>The power of the Gospels is as strong as ever</u>. We can put our faith in them and the Lord they describe.

But you don't have to be an anti-supernatural critic to notice that occasionally one Gospel will say something that another seems to contradict. What about those cases?

Disagreements among the Gospels

In the Gospels we have four separate books looking at the same subject, the life of Jesus. As a result, it is not surprising that they don't always describe events or speeches exactly the same way. But do the Gospels really disagree? Or do they just *appear* to disagree?

Imagine that a crime was committed at the intersection of two streets. Four people (each standing on one of the corners) happened to see the crime taking place. If you asked these witnesses about it later, do you think they would describe the crime exactly the same way? No, each would tell the particular details that he or she remembers. Their reports would not necessarily be in disagreement, though they would not be the same.

It's similar for the Gospels. They do not *contradict* each other; they *balance* each other, looking at their subject from different angles. The Holy Spirit who inspired these books is a Spirit of truth, and He preserved the accuracy of the four accounts (*John 14:26; 16:13*).

Let's consider several of the apparent contradictions among the Gospels. Usually a little study—or just plain common sense—suggests a resolution.[9]

1. Why do Matthew and Luke present a different family heritage for Jesus? See *Matthew 1:17-18; Luke 3:23-38*.

   Suggested solution: It may be that Matthew gives the family line through Jesus' legal father, Joseph, while Luke gives the line through Jesus' mother, Mary.

2. Why do Matthew and Luke describe Jesus' temptations in different orders? See *Matthew 4:3-10; Luke 4:3-12*.

   Suggested solution: Possibly Matthew gives the temptations in the order in which they actually happened, while Luke gives them in a topical order to make a point.

3. Why does Matthew say that Jesus gave the Sermon on the Mount on a mountain, while Luke says He gave it on a level place? See *Matthew 5:1; Luke 6:17*.

   Suggested solution: Likely Jesus stood on a level spot to speak to a crowd who were seated around Him on a mountain.

4. Why does Matthew say that Jesus cast demons out of two men in the area of Gerasa, while Mark and Luke mention only one man? See *Matthew 8:28-34; Mark 5:1-20; Luke 8:26-39*.

   Suggested solution: If there were two, then that means there was also one. No contradiction here!

5. Why does Matthew say that the mother of James and John came to Jesus to make a request on her sons' behalf, while Mark says that James and John themselves came to Jesus? See *Matthew 20:20; Mark 10:35*.

   Suggested solution: No doubt the mother came with the two disciples. She may have spoken first, followed by James and John.

6. Why does Luke say that Jesus healed a blind man as He entered Jericho, while Matthew and Mark say that such a healing took place as Jesus left Jericho? See *Matthew 20:29-34; Mark 10:46-52; Luke 18:35-43*.

NOTES

NOTES

Suggested solution: Possibly Jesus performed one healing miracle before entering Jericho and then performed a similar miracle upon leaving the city. Or possibly the confusion is due to the fact that there were two Jerichos, an old one and a new one. Jesus may have healed the blind man while leaving one Jericho and entering the other.

7. Why does Mark say that Jesus cursed a fig tree before cleansing the temple, while Matthew says Jesus cursed the tree after cleansing the temple? See *Matthew 21:12-19; Mark 11:12-14, 20-24*.

   Suggested solution: Jesus made two trips to the temple on two separate days, and He cursed the fig tree on His way to the temple the second time.

8. Why does Matthew say that both criminals crucified with Jesus mocked Him, while Luke says that one mocked Him and the other repented? See *Matthew 27:44; Luke 23:39, 42*.

   Suggested solution: Likely both men mocked Jesus at first, then, after a time, one of them repented.

9. Why does Mark say that Mary came to Jesus' tomb at dawn, while John says it was still dark? See *Mark 16:1-2; John 20:1*.

   Suggested solution: Possibly Mary came to the tomb alone when it was still dark, then came a second time with other women after sunrise.

10. Why does Luke say that Jesus gave up His spirit to the Father on the cross, yet we read in John that the recently resurrected Jesus said He had not yet ascended to His Father? See *Luke 23:46; John 20:17*.

    Suggested solution: The day Jesus died, His Spirit went to be with the Father. His resurrected body and his Spirit did unite at the beginning of His 40 days on earth before His ascension.

What's remarkable about the Gospels is not that they present a scattering of apparent discrepancies. What's remarkable is how much in agreement these four documents—having been written by different men at different times—really are. We can trust the Gospels and believe in the one Jesus they reveal to us.

Questions

If you were ever to encounter someone who argued that the Gospels contain falsehood, how would you react?

Do any apparent contradictions among the Gospels trouble you? If so, which ones and why? What can you do to resolve these issues in your own mind?

How will you preach on questionable passages in your new church?

Chapter Four
The Gospel of the King: An Overview and Outline of Matthew

The Gospel of Matthew is a noble beginning to the Bible's description of Jesus. Here we see Jesus as the Messiah and King of the Jews.

> Key verse: *"They put up over His head the accusation written against Him: THIS IS JESUS THE KING OF THE JEWS"* (Matthew 27:37).

In fact, this Gospel shows Jesus as the King of the universe. <u>All people ought to know and obey Him</u>. One New Testament scholar wrote:

> *Matthew seeks to show that Jesus is the finale of salvation history. God's purpose to bring salvation to the world finds its conclusion in him. The prophecies have been fulfilled! If Jesus is truly the promised Messiah, then the church, made up of both Jews and Gentiles, is the authentic people of God. God's plan of salvation for the world is now going forward, not through the synagogue but through the new people of God made up of people from all nations. This is the critical point at issue for Matthew and his community.*
>
> *Seen in this light, the questions Matthew answers are just as profound and important today. What is God's purpose and goal for this world? What sets apart the true followers of God? What must people do to find salvation? The First Gospel rejects any claim to truth which does not find its center in the kingdom of heaven beginning through the life, death, and resurrection of Jesus the Messiah. All other worldviews, religions, and philosophies fall short.*[10]

The Author of the Gospel of Matthew

None of the four Gospels specifically name their authors. So, how do we know who wrote them? There are two lines of evidence.

1. **Evidence of the author's identity from outside the Bible**

    Early Christian writings (apart from the Bible) give the names of the authors of the Gospels. These sources may not always be reliable, but probably in many cases they are correct.

    In the case of the First Gospel, a writer named Papias (who lived about AD 70–163) is reported to have said, "Matthew composed his Gospel in the Hebrew language, and everyone translated as they were able."

2. **Evidence of the author's identity from the Bible itself**

    The Bible gives us clues to the identity of the Gospels' authors.
    The Gospel of Matthew clues us in to an author who was a Jew living in Palestine (the name for Israel at that time).

    A. The author knew the geography of Palestine well (see *Matthew 2:1; 8:5; 20:29; 26:6*).

    B. The author was familiar with Jewish history and customs (see *Matthew 1:18-19; 2:1; 14:1; 26:3; 27:2*).

    C. The author knew the Hebrew Scriptures (Old Testament) well (see *Matthew 1:2-6, 22, 23; 2:6; 4:14-16; 12:17-21; 13:35; 21:4; 27:9*).

    D. The author used words in ways that Jews from Palestine often did (see *Matthew 2:20; 4:5; 5:35; 10:6; 15:24; 17:24-27; 18:17; 27:53*).

    None of this identifies Matthew as the writer beyond all doubt. But there are a couple of other clues.

    E. The author refers four times to the town of Capernaum. This was Matthew's hometown (see *Matthew 4:13; 8:5; 11:23; 17:24*).

    F. The author refers to money more often than did the other Gospel writers. Matthew was a tax collector (see *Matthew 6:24; 20:1-16; 21:12; 22:19; 25:14-30; 26:9; 27:6-7; 28:12-15*).

NOTES

Taken with the reports from early Christian writers, these clues from the First Gospel give us confidence in identifying Matthew as the author.

The Life of Matthew

Before becoming a follower of Jesus, Matthew (also called Levi) collected taxes for the Romans. He worked in the town of Capernaum, which was located in Galilee (northern Israel). If he was like other tax collectors of his time, he made himself wealthy by taking more from the people than they owed. He was a hated member of his society. Yet he met Jesus—and everything changed for him.

Jesus used the occasion of calling Matthew to teach about His own role as Savior for sinners.

> *As Jesus passed on from there, He saw a man named Matthew sitting at the tax office. And He said to him, "Follow Me." So he arose and followed Him. Now it happened, as Jesus sat at the table in the house, that behold, many tax collectors and sinners came and sat down with Him and His disciples. And when the Pharisees saw it, they said to His disciples, "Why does your Teacher eat with tax collectors and sinners?" When Jesus heard that, He said to them, "Those who are well have no need of a physician, but those who are sick. But go and learn what this means: 'I desire mercy and not sacrifice.' For I did not come to call the righteous, but sinners, to repentance" (Matthew 9:9-13).*

NOTES

According to tradition, after Jesus' death, Matthew was involved in missionary work and may have been killed for his faith in Ethiopia or Persia. His writing of the First Gospel was his most enduring legacy.

The Date and Place for the Writing of the Gospel of Matthew

History supplies some evidence for the latest time when the Gospel of Matthew would have been written.

Jesus told in advance that the temple would be destroyed (*Matthew 24:1-2*). In fact, in AD 70, the Romans destroyed not only the temple, but also much of the city of Jerusalem. Yet, the Gospel of Matthew seems to imply that, at the time it was written, this terrible event had not yet happened.

1. The author speaks of Jerusalem as if it were still standing (see *Matthew 4:5; 27:53*).

2. The author speaks of the customs of the Jews as continuing till "this day" (see *Matthew 27:8; 28:15*).

On this basis, most Bible scholars agree that the Gospel of Matthew was written before AD 70, probably between AD 60 and 65. Matthew may have still been living in Jerusalem at the time, though there is no way to be sure about that.

The Original Readers of the Gospel of Matthew

While all four Gospels reflect the Jewish origin of the Messiah, the Gospel of Matthew does so more clearly than any of the others. This makes sense, because Matthew was a Jew. It also makes sense to conclude that he saw himself as writing primarily to Jews.

Matthew used common Jewish terms:

1. He used the term "kingdom of heaven" or "kingdom of God" thirty-seven times.

2. He used the term "Son of David" for Jesus nine times.

3. He referred to Jerusalem as "the holy city" or the "city of the great King."

Also, he referred often to Jewish heroes (including Moses, David, and the Messiah), customs (the law, Sabbath rest, religious cleanness), and landmarks (the temple). Since he usually did not bother to explain what these things were, he must have assumed that his readers would already know about them.

Finally, the author referred directly or indirectly to the Hebrew Scriptures (Old Testament) over one hundred times. In particular, he tried to show how Jesus fulfilled Old Testament prophecy of the Messiah.

Ten of the "Fulfillment" Passages in Matthew		
Prophecy	**Prophecy**	**Fulfillment**
Virgin birth	*Isaiah 7:14*	*Matthew 1:22-23*
Escape to Egypt	*Hosea 11:1*	*Matthew 2:15*
Children murdered in Bethlehem	*Jeremiah 31:15*	*Matthew 2:17-18*
Childhood in Nazareth	possibly *Isaiah 11:1*	*Matthew 2:23*
Ministry in Galilee	*Isaiah 9:2*	*Matthew 4:14-16*
Healing disease	*Isaiah 53:4*	*Matthew 8:17*
Role of Servant	*Isaiah 42:2*	*Matthew 12:17-21*
Speaking in parables	*Psalm 78:2;* *2 Chronicles 29:30*	*Matthew 13:35*
Entering Jerusalem as humble king	*Zechariah 9:9*	*Matthew 21:4-5*
Betrayed for thirty pieces of silver	*Zechariah 11:12-13*	*Matthew 27:9-10*

The original readers of the Gospel were Jews. But through them, the Gospel has come to the whole world and blessed us all.

The Purposes of the Gospel of Matthew

Of course, the Gospel of Matthew is intended to show its readers who Jesus is. But if we look more closely at it, we realize that it also has some other purposes.

1. To prove to Jews that Jesus is the Messiah
   For example, the genealogy of Jesus in chapter one proves that Jesus is descended from King David.

2. To describe the Kingdom of God
   The Gospel's many references to the kingdom reveal that it is present in Jesus, even though Jesus does not yet reign on earth.

3. To explain the origin of the Church
   This is the only Gospel to refer to the Church (*Matthew 16:18; 18:17*). Despite the Jewish quality of this Gospel, it also shows non-Jews coming to believe in Jesus the role and need for His Church.

4. To show Jesus as a Teacher
   All four Gospels present a mix of Jesus' words and deeds. But the Gospel of Matthew emphasizes Jesus' words. In particular, it contains five major collections of Jesus' teachings.

Five Major Teachings by Jesus in the Gospel of Matthew

Teaching	Reference
The Sermon on the Mount	*Matthew 5-7*
Warning about opposition	*Matthew 10*
A collection of parables about the Kingdom	*Matthew 13*
Parables and teachings about humility	*Matthew 18*
Teaching about the end times	*Matthew 23-25*

NOTES

5. <u>To teach the church</u>
The Gospel presents major teachings by Jesus and gives the church its "Great Commission" (*Matthew 28:18-20*).

An Outline of the Gospel of Matthew

1. <u>The Birth of Jesus, the Messiah</u>

    A. From the line of King David (*1:1-17*)

    B. Born to Mary and Joseph (*1:18-25*)

    C. Visited by wise men (*2:1-12*)

    D. Taken to Egypt (*2:13-18*)

    E. Raised in Nazareth (*2:19-23*)

2. <u>Jesus Begins His Ministry</u>

    A. Baptized by John the Baptist (*3:1-7*)

    B. Tempted by the devil (*4:1-11*)

    C. Choosing His disciples (*4:12-25*)

    D. The Sermon on the Mount (*5:1-7:29*)

3. <u>Jesus' First Miracles</u>

    A. His power over leprosy, demons, and a storm (*8:1-34*)

    B. His power over disease and death (*9:1-34*)

4. <u>Jesus Teaches about the Kingdom</u>

    A. The workers in the Kingdom (*9:35-10:42*)

    B. People's responses to the Kingdom (*11:1-12:50*)

    C. Parables about the Kingdom (*13:1-52*)

    D. The prophets of the Kingdom are rejected (*13:53-14:12*)

5. <u>More Miracles of Jesus… and a Confession</u>

    A. Feeding five thousand and walking on water (*14:13-36*)

    B. Confronting traditions (*15:1-20*)

    C. Healing a Canaanite woman's daughter (*15:21-28*)

    D. Feeding four thousand (*15:29-39*)

    E. A sign for the Pharisees and Sadducees (*16:1-12*)

    F. The confession of Peter (*16:13-20*)

6. How to Follow Jesus

    A. Jesus headed to the cross (*16:19-28*)

    B. Jesus is transformed (*17:1-23*)

    C. Paying taxes to the temple (*17:24-27*)

    D. Being truly great and forgiving others (*18:1-35*)

    E. Having a good marriage and childlike faith (*19:1-15*)

    F. Giving up possessions (*19:16-30*)

    G. Being last to be first (*20:1-28*)

7. Passion Week

    A. Healing the blind and riding into Jerusalem (*20:29-21:11*)

    B. Clearing the temple and condemning the religious leaders (*21:12-22:14*)

    C. Teaching on taxes, marriage, and loving God (*21:15-46*)

    D. Condemning the religious leaders (*23:1-38*)

    E. Teaching about His second coming (*24:1-25:46*)

8. Jesus Is Tried and Crucified

    A. Anointed and betrayed (*26:1-16*)

    B. Sharing His Last Supper (*26:17-35*)

    C. Prayer in Gethsemane, arrest, and trial (*26:36-68*)

    D. Left by His disciples (*26:69-27:10*)

    E. Tried and convicted by Pilate (*27:11-31*)

    F. Crucified and buried in a guarded tomb (*27:32-61*)

NOTES

9. <u>Jesus Is Alive</u>

   A. An empty tomb (*28:1-10*)

   B. The false report of the guards (*28:11-15*)

   C. Jesus' final instructions (*28:16-20*)

Assignment: Read the Gospel of Matthew.

Questions

If you were a Jewish person who had never heard of Jesus before, and you were reading this Gospel for the first time, what do you think you might conclude about who Jesus is?

What major themes do you observe in the teachings of Jesus recorded in the Gospel of Matthew?

What does the Gospel say about the church that is important for pastors and church planters to know?

Suggestions on How to Preach through the Gospel of Matthew

As church planters you will need to preach through the Gospel of Matthew at some point. Consider the following sermon topics featuring highlights from the Gospel.

"Wise Men Worship the King"
Passage: *Matthew 2:1-12*
Key point: Jesus deserves all our worship.

"Have the Characteristics of a Christian"
Passage: *Matthew 5:1-16*
Key point: What is on the inside should show on the outside.

"Jesus Teaches about Prayer"
Passage: *Matthew 6:5-15*
Key point: Prayer is a relationship with God.

"A Roman Centurion Shows Great Faith"
Passage: *Matthew 8:5-13*
Key point: Jesus' miracles are for anyone who believes.

"Jesus Describes the Cost of Discipleship"
Passage: *Matthew 10:32-42*
Key point: Following Jesus takes courage and sacrifice.

"Jesus Teaches about Forgiveness"
Passage: *Matthew 18:15-35*
Key point: Forgive others as God forgives you.

"Jesus Teaches about Loving Others"
Passage: *Matthew 25:31-46*
Key point: When we help others, we are serving Jesus.

"Jesus' Death Cannot Go Unnoticed"
Passage: *Matthew 27:45-54*
Key point: Jesus' sacrifice opens our way to God.

"Jesus Rises from the Dead"
Passage: *Matthew 28:10*
Key point: Jesus has conquered death so we can live.

"Jesus Gives the Great Commission"
Passage: *Matthew 28:16-20*
Key point: We are called to go and make disciples.

NOTES

Chapter Five
The Gospel of the Servant: An Overview and Outline of Mark

If we were honest, we would admit that we'd rather be served by others, not be a servant. It's the same for everybody. Yet Jesus showed us a radically different way, and this difference comes out clearly in the Gospel of Mark.

Key verse: *"For even the Son of Man did not come to be served, but to serve, and to give His life a ransom for many"* (Mark 10:45).

As one scholar wrote,

Mark's Gospel reminds us that the goal of the Christian life is not to find security or self-fulfillment. Following Jesus is responding to a radical call to commitment, taking up our crosses and following him. The gospel holds no promise for those who are seeking power and wealth and fame and prestige. To be first, Jesus says, you must be last. To be a leader, you must become a slave. To live, you must die.[11]

This clear, active, and powerful Gospel portrays a Jesus who leads the way to suffering and to servanthood—but also to glory.

The Author of the Gospel of Mark

1. **Evidence of the author's identity from outside the Bible**

    A. Early Christian writers identified Mark as the author of this Gospel.

    B. The second-century writer Papias is reported to have said, "Mark became the interpreter of Peter." This is often taken to mean that Mark relied on Peter as his primary source of information for the Gospel. Interestingly, the outline of Mark's Gospel follows the outline of Peter's sermon to Cornelius (*Acts 10:34-43*).

    C. Several other authors from the second century referred to Mark as the author of the Second Gospel.

2. **Evidence of the author's identity from the Bible itself**

    A. A strange little incident in the Gospel may be a clue to Mark's authorship of this Gospel. Only in this Gospel do we learn about a "certain young man" who followed Jesus from the site of the Last Supper to the

Garden of Gethsemane (*Mark 14:51-52*). It may be that the author of the Second Gospel didn't name this "young man" because it was the author himself. And there is some evidence that the Last Supper may have been held in Mark's home (*Acts 12:12*).

B. There is no compelling reason not to believe the early testimony of the church that Mark wrote this Gospel.

The Life of Mark

1. Mark (also known as John Mark) was not one of the twelve disciples. But he had a close relationship with early Christian leaders and saw many of the great events of the early church up close.

2. As we have seen, the Last Supper may have been held in his home, and he may have been the young man who followed Jesus to Gethsemane (see *Mark 14:51-52*).

3. His home was a gathering place for the Christians after Jesus' death (see *Acts 12:12*).

4. He was a cousin of Barnabas (see *Colossians 4:10*).

5. Peter called Mark his "son," probably meaning that he had led Mark to faith in Jesus or had served as his spiritual mentor (see *1 Peter 5:13*).

6. Paul and Barnabas took the young Mark with them when they left on their missionary journey. In the midst of this journey, however, Mark left them—perhaps because he had lost his courage in the face of opposition. This later led to an argument between Paul and Barnabas, with Paul no longer being willing to trust Mark (see *Acts 12:25; 13:5, 13; 15:36-41*).

7. In time, Paul came to consider Mark a valuable and reliable fellow servant of Jesus (see *Colossians 4:10-11; 2 Timothy 4:11; Philemon 1:23-24*).

The Date and Place for the Writing of the Gospel of Mark

Like Matthew, Mark appears to have been written while Jerusalem was still standing and the temple was still operating. So this means it must have been written before AD 70, when the Romans destroyed Jerusalem.

Mark was reportedly with Peter in Rome during the days leading up to the apostle's death in about AD 64. Mark may have completed this Gospel in Rome either shortly before or shortly after Peter's death.

The Original Readers of the Gospel of Mark

1. The clues in the Gospels suggest that Mark wrote for Gentile Christians (especially Romans), not Jews.

NOTES

2. He did not assume that the readers knew the Hebrew Scriptures, and in fact he quoted only one Old Testament passage (see *Mark 1:2-3*).

3. He explained Jewish customs and geography (see *Mark 7:2-4; 13:3; 14:12*).

4. He left out Jesus' instructions to the disciples not to preach to Gentiles (see *Mark 6:7-11*; compare *Matthew 10:5-6*).

5. In the middle of the first century, the church was expanding rapidly throughout the Roman Empire. Mark wrote primarily for these believers—as well as for everyone else.

The Purposes of the Gospel of Mark

1. To preserve the facts about Jesus

   - With Peter and other eyewitnesses of Jesus passing from the scene, Mark no doubt recognized the importance of writing down the stories of Jesus' words and deeds before the accounts of them were lost. If he was indeed the first Gospel writer, as many scholars now think, Mark started the trend of writing down the Jesus story.

2. To encourage worried believers

   - Mark wrote at a time when Roman Christians were beginning to experience persecution. His description of a Savior who triumphed through mistreatment and even murder would have given them courage.

R. A. Guelich says,

The pastoral concern was foremost in Mark's mind as he wrote "the gospel concerning Jesus Messiah, Son of God." He wanted to address a community under duress that may well have given rise to questions about who Jesus really was and the nature of the kingdom he had come to inaugurate. This Gospel offered a renewed basis for their faith, made clear the trials and tribulations along the journey of that faith, and offered the hope of the kingdom future when... God's salvation would make all things right.[12]

An Outline of the Gospel of Mark

1. Jesus' Ministry Begins

   A. John the Baptist prepares the way (*1:1-8*)

   B. Jesus is baptized, tempted, and chooses disciples (*1:9-20*)

   C. Jesus heals a leper and a paralyzed man (*1:21-2:12*)

   D. Jesus calls Matthew and confronts the Pharisees (*2:13-3:6*)

2. Jesus Teaches in Galilee

   A. The crowds gather, and He chooses more disciples (*3:7-19*)

   B. Jesus says you are for Him or against Him (*3:20-35*)

   C. Jesus tells stories of a sower, lamp, and seeds (*4:1-34*)

   D. Jesus calms a storm on the Sea (*4:35-41*)

   E. Jesus heals a man with demons, a sick woman, and raises a dead girl (*5:1-43*)

   F. Jesus is rejected in His hometown, Nazareth (*6:1-6*)

3. Jesus Expands His Ministry

   A. Jesus sends out the Twelve (*6:7-13*)

   B. John the Baptist is beheaded (*6:14-29*)

   C. Jesus feeds five thousand (*6:30-44*)

   D. Jesus walks on the Sea (*6:45-56*)

   E. Jesus tells what is clean and unclean (*7:1-23*)

   F. Jesus heals in Phoenicia and in the Decapolis (*7:24-37*)

   G. Jesus feeds four thousand and heals a blind man (*8:1-26*)

4. Jesus Shows His Identity and His Mission

   A. Peter says Jesus is the Christ (*8:27-30*)

   B. Jesus says following Him means denying yourself (*8:31-9:1*)

   C. The disciples see Jesus transformed (*9:2-13*)

5. Jesus Finds Belief and Unbelief

   A. A father believes and his son is healed (*9:14-32*)

   B. The disciples argue over greatness and glory (*9:33-41*)

   C. Have childlike faith and avoid divorce (*9:42-10:16*)

   D. Give up your possessions and your position (*10:17-45*)

   E. Blind Bartimaeus believes and sees (*10:46-52*)

NOTES

6. <u>Jesus Comes to Jerusalem</u>

    A. Crowds cheer as Jesus enters Jerusalem (*11:1-11*)

    B. Jesus clears the temple and shows His authority (*11:12-12:12*)

    C. Jesus teaches about taxes, marriage, and loving God (*12:13-44*)

    D. Jesus talks about His return (*13:1-37*)

7. <u>Jesus Sacrifices Himself for Us</u>

    A. Jesus is anointed and betrayed (*14:1-11*)

    B. Jesus eats the Last Supper, prays, and is arrested (*14:12-65*)

    C. Peter denies Jesus (*14:66-72*)

    D. Jesus is tried, convicted, crucified, and buried (*15:1-47*)

    E. Jesus rises on the third day (*16:1-8*)

    F. Jesus commissions His disciples and goes to heaven (*16:9-20*)*

*Note: The best early versions of the Gospel of Mark do not include these verses. These verses were probably added later to give the Gospel a stronger sense of completion.

Assignment: Read the Gospel of Mark.

Questions

It is often pointed out that this Gospel features especially vivid, active storytelling. Which story in the Gospel is particularly memorable to you, and why?

One scholar wrote two books about the Gospel of Mark, one called The Servant Who Rules (about *Mark 1-8*) and the other called The Ruler Who Serves (about *Mark 9-16*).[13] What evidence do you find in this Gospel that Jesus is indeed a Servant-King?

How can the Gospel of Mark help persecuted believers today?

How does Mark call you to a higher level of living in Jesus as a church planter?

Suggestions on How to Preach through the Gospel of Mark   NOTES

"John the Baptist Prepares the Way for Jesus"
Passage: *Mark 1:1-8, 14*
Key point: We are called to repent and believe the Good News.

"Jesus Heals the Paralyzed Man"
Passage: *Mark 2:1-12*
Key point: Jesus can heal physically and spiritually.

"The Parable of the Four Soils"
Passage: *Mark 4:1-25*
Key point: Not everyone allows the Gospel to grow in their hearts.

"Jesus Feeds More than Five Thousand People"
Passage: *Mark 6:30-44*
Key point: Jesus can meet all our needs.

"Peter Says Jesus Is the Messiah"
Passage: *Mark 8:27-9:8*
Key point: Each one of us must decide who Jesus really is.

"The Cost of Following Jesus"
Passage: *Mark 10:17-31*
Key point: We must make sacrifices to follow Jesus.

"People Praise Jesus as He Rides into Jerusalem"
Passage: *Mark 11:1-11*
Key point: Jesus is worthy of our praise.

"Jesus Predicts That Peter Will Deny Him"
Passage: *Mark 14:27-31, 66-72*
Key point: At times we are all guilty of denying Jesus.

"Jesus Cries Out to God"
Passage: *Mark 15:33-37*
Key point: Jesus felt forsaken as He sacrificed Himself for us.

"The Stone Is Rolled Away"
Passage: *Mark 16:1-8*
Key point: The empty tomb proves Jesus has risen from the dead.

Chapter Six
The Gospel of the Son of Man: An Overview and Outline of Luke

The Gospel of Luke is the longest Gospel, giving us the widest variety of miracle stories and teachings by Jesus. It is also the only Gospel with a sequel. The book of Acts continues the Jesus story into the times of the early church (see *Luke 1:1-4; Acts 1:1-3*).

The author of the Third Gospel was a careful historian who wanted to preserve accounts of the historical activities of Jesus. Here we see Jesus as a flesh-and-blood man (though also the divine Savior), who performed real miracles in the real world. He was the Son of Man living among men and women.

> Key verse: *"for the Son of Man has come to seek and to save that which was lost"* (Luke 19:10).

In this Gospel, we learn about the blessings of salvation through Jesus. We learn that Jesus' healing and preaching were especially for the poor and needy. The grace of God, revealed in Jesus, is given to those who may seem least worthy of it, such as sinful women and greedy tax collectors.

New Testament scholar F. W. Burnett wrote,

> *Luke's Gospel is pastoral, theological and historical. The reality of God's plan impacts how individuals see themselves and the community to which they belong. Old barriers of race are removed. New hope abounds. The message of Jesus is one of hope and transformation. Anyone, Jew or Gentile, can belong to the new community. At the center is Jesus, the promised Messiah-Lord, who sits at God's right hand exercising authority from above. He will return one day and all are accountable to him. His life, ministry and resurrection/ascension show he is worthy of trust. Just as he has inaugurated the fulfillment of God's promises, so he will bring them to completion. In the meantime, being a disciple is not easy, but it is full of rich blessing which transcends anything else this life can offer. This is the reassurance about salvation which Luke offers to Theophilus and others like him.*[14]

The Author of the Gospel of Luke

1. **Evidence of the author's identity from outside the Bible**

    - Several early Christian writers, including Justin Martyr (about AD 100–165) and Tertullian (about AD 160–220), identified Luke as the author of the Third Gospel. In fact, no early Christian writing suggests anybody else as the author.

2. **Evidence of the author's identity from the Bible itself**

    A. The author of the Third Gospel implies that he was not an eyewitness to the ministry of Jesus (*Luke 1:1-4*). Thus he was not one of the original disciples.

    B. He wrote in an elegant Greek style, as would be expected of a well-educated person such as a doctor.

    C. The Gospel's special interest in Gentiles coming to believe in Jesus would make sense if the author himself were a Gentile Christian.

    D. All of this is consistent with Luke being the author of this Gospel.

The Life of Luke

Luke was a doctor. Probably he was someone whom Paul met while on one of his missionary journeys and led to faith in Jesus, though we don't know exactly where or when this happened.

Colossians 4:10-14 seems to suggest that Luke was not Jewish. If so, he was the only Gentile to write a book of the New Testament.

Since Paul seems to have had an ongoing medical condition (*2 Corinthians 12:7-10; Galatians 6:11*), and suffered injuries during his travels (*2 Corinthians 11:23-33*), Luke may have decided to go along with him to serve as his personal physician as well as a fellow missionary. He played an important, though supporting role in the growth of the early Christian church.

1. The sections of the book of Acts that use the word "we" show that the author traveled extensively with Paul and even stuck with him during his imprisonment (see *Acts 16:10-17; 20:5-15; 21:1-18; 27:1-28:16*).

2. Luke was a physician, and Paul was fond of him (see *Colossians 4:14*).

3. Paul considered Luke to be a faithful fellow worker (see *2 Timothy 4:11; Philemon 1:24*).

4. Early Christian tradition says that, after Paul died, Luke settled in Philippi and eventually died there.

The Date and Place for the Writing of the Gospel of Luke

The book of Acts ends with Paul in prison in Rome, probably in AD 62 (*Acts 28:16-31*). This means Luke and Acts were both probably finished at that time. It is easy to

NOTES

imagine Luke writing these books in Rome as he waited for Paul's legal process to work its way to completion.

The Original Readers of the Gospel of Luke

Luke addressed both Luke and Acts to a man named Theophilus. We know little about this person. Probably he was a Gentile and a new follower of Jesus. Since Luke called him "most excellent" (*Luke 1:3*), he was no doubt a prominent person in the society of that day. He may have asked Luke to write these two books and promised to pay him for them.

Surely Luke knew that the books would be read by far more people than just Theophilus. He was writing to Gentile believers in general.

The Purposes of the Gospel of Luke

1. <u>To establish a firm historical foundation for the Gospel</u>

   - Luke himself said to his patron, *"Inasmuch as many have taken in hand to set in order a narrative of those things which have been fulfilled among us, just as those who from the beginning were eyewitnesses and ministers of the word delivered them to us, it seemed good to me also, having had perfect understanding of all things from the very first, to write to you an orderly account, most excellent Theophilus, that you may know the certainty of those things in which you were instructed"* (*Luke 1:1-4*).

2. <u>To defend Christianity against its opponents</u>

   A. At the time Luke wrote, Christianity was receiving criticism from the Jewish community and from some parts of the Gentile world. Some of the things being said about the new faith were not true. Therefore, everyone needed to know what the "Jesus faith" was really all about.

   B. The New Testament scholar Mark Strauss sums up Luke's second purpose like this:

   Luke writes to confirm the gospel. To demonstrate the authenticity of the claims of Christianity. This confirmation certainly relates to accusations made by the church's Jewish opponents. The author takes pains to show that Jesus is the Jewish Messiah, that it was God's purpose for him to suffer, die, and rise again, that the mission to the Gentiles was ordained and instigated by God, and that Paul is not a renegade Jew but a faithful servant of the Lord. There are also indications that Luke seeks to deflect Roman criticism. Both Jesus (in the Gospel) and Paul (in Acts) are repeatedly confirmed as innocent of Roman charges. Christianity is not a dangerous new religion but the fulfillment of Judaism (a legal religion in Roman eyes), the consummation of God's plan of salvation.[15]

An Outline of the Gospel of Luke

1. <u>The Birth of Jesus, the Savior</u>

    A. Luke's reason for writing (*1:1-4*)

    B. The announcements of two births (*1:5-56*)

    C. The birth of John the Baptist (*1:57-80*)

    D. The birth and childhood of Jesus (*2:1-52*)

2. <u>Jesus Gets Ready for Ministry</u>

    A. The ministry of John the Baptist (*3:1-20*)

    B. Jesus' baptism and a list of his ancestors (*3:21-37*)

    C. Jesus' temptations and His rejection at Nazareth (*4:1-30*)

3. <u>Jesus and His Ministry in Galilee</u>

    A. Jesus' healings and the call of His disciples (*4:31-6:16*)

    B. Jesus' teachings on love and judgment (*6:17-49*)

    C. Faith and the forgiving of sin (*7:1-50*)

    D. Stories, a calmed storm, and two healed women (*8:1-56*)

4. <u>Jesus' Identity and His Mission</u>

    A. The twelve disciples are sent out (*9:1-9*)

    B. Feeding the five thousand (*9:10-17*)

    C. Peter's confession, and Jesus is transformed (*9:18-36*)

    D. The cost of believing (*9:37-62*)

    E. Requirements for missionaries (*10:1-42*)

5. <u>Jesus' Teachings and His Followers</u>

    A. How to pray and to cast out demons (*11:1-27*)

    B. Woes and warnings (*11:28-13:35*)

    C. Descriptions of the kingdom in parables (*14:1-18:14*)

NOTES

        D. Childlike faith and restored sight (*18:15-43*)

        E. A repentant tax collector and the kingdom (*19:1-27*)

    6. <u>Jesus' Final Week</u>

        A. Jesus enters Jerusalem and clears the temple (*19:28-48*)

        B. Jesus teaches in the temple (*20:1-21:4*)

        C. Signs of Jesus' return (*21:5-38*)

        D. Jesus is betrayed, the Last Supper, and His arrest (*22:1-53*)

        E. Denied, tried, and sentenced to death (*22:54-23:25*)

        F. Crucified and buried (*23:26-56*)

    7. <u>Jesus' Resurrection</u>

        A. The empty tomb (*24:1-12*)

        B. Jesus appears to disciples on the road to Emmaus (*24:13-35*)

        C. Jesus appears to the eleven disciples and goes up to heaven (*24:36-53*)

Assignment: Read the Gospel of Luke.

Questions

What evidence do you find in the Gospel of Luke that the author was concerned about being historically accurate and precise?

What passages in this Gospel emphasize to you the compassion that God has for the poor, the needy, the overlooked and outcasts?

With Luke's emphasis on Jesus and His humanity, how can you emphasize His perfect humanity in church planting?

Assignment: Read the book of Acts.

Question

How does the book of Acts expand the image of Jesus that we find in Luke?

Suggestions on How to Preach through the Gospel of Luke

"Jesus Is Born"
Passage: *Luke 2:1-20*
Key point: Jesus' birth is good news for everyone.

"Satan Tempts Jesus"
Passage: Luke *4:1-13*
Key point: Jesus faced temptations, just like we do.

"Jesus Calls His Disciples"
Passage: *Luke 5:1-11*
Key point: A follower of Jesus is a fisher of men.

"Jesus Says to Love Your Enemies"
Passage: *Luke 6:27-36*
Key point: Do to others as you would want them to do to you.

"Jesus Performs Miracles"
Passage: *Luke 8:40-56*
Key point: Faith is the most important part of healing.

"The Parable of the Good Samaritan"
Passage: *Luke 10:25-37*
Key point: Because we love God, we can also love the outcasts.

"The Parable of the Lost Son"
Passage: *Luke 15:11-31*
Key point: God is waiting for all of us to come home to Him.

"Jesus Celebrates the Last Supper"
Passage: *Luke 22:7-26*
Key point: Jesus gave everything for us.

"Jesus Dies between Two Thieves"
Passage: *Luke 23:32-43*
Key point: Jesus will forgive and save us if we ask Him.

"Two Disciples See the Risen Jesus"
Passage: *Luke 24:13-35*
Key point: Jesus opens the Scriptures to those who will listen.

Chapter Seven
The Gospel of the Son of God: An Overview and Outline of John

We saw in the previous chapter that the Gospel of Luke emphasizes the actions of Jesus in real history. He is the Son of Man who has come to save fellow human beings from the sin we suffer from in this world.

But there is another side to Jesus. He is not only a man; He is also God. And that's why the Gospel of John focuses on Jesus as the Son of God.[16]

> Key verse: *"For God so loved the world that He gave His only begotten Son, that whoever believes in Him should not perish but have everlasting life"* (*John 3:16*).

As we leave the first three Gospels and enter the world of John, we feel that what we are reading is the same and yet different. There is a reason why Matthew, Mark, and Luke are called the Synoptic Gospels—they really do tend to look at things generally the same way. John is clearly different.

It's not that we're meeting a different Jesus in the Gospel of John. It's that John wrote a fresh Gospel with his own special writing style and with intentions that were more theological. The Gospel of John beautifully completes the description of Jesus that was started in the first three Gospels. It presents us with a God-man who challenges each of us to believe in Him.

The Author of the Gospel of John

1. **Evidence of the author's identity from outside the Bible**

    Early Christian writers identified John as the author of this book. For example, Polycarp (about AD 69–155), who was a disciple of John, said that John wrote the Fourth Gospel.

2. **Evidence of the author's identity from the Bible itself**

    Like the other three Gospel writers, this writer does not name himself. Yet he leaves us with little doubt about his identity.

    The author calls himself "the disciple whom Jesus loved" (see *John 13:23; 19:26; 20:2; 21:7, 20*).

    The author clearly states that "this is the disciple who testifies of these things, and wrote these things" (*John 21:24*).

He must have been one of the twelve disciples and probably one of the three who were closest to Jesus: Peter, James, and John (*Matthew 17:1*). Because of the way Peter is referred to in *John 21:20*, the writer could not have been Peter. And James died too early to have written this Gospel (*Acts 12:1-2*). So it must have been John.

The Life of John

Who was John? This apostle was the most prominent of the Gospel writers and one of the best-known figures in all of early Christianity.

1. John was born in the village of Bethsaida, on the shore of the Sea of Galilee. His father was named Zebedee and his mother was named Salome. His brother (who, like John, became an apostle) was named James. The family apparently owned a fishing business (see *Matthew 4:21; 10:2; 27:56* [compare *Mark 15:40*] *Mark 1:19; 3:17; 10:35*).

2. Jesus calls John and James to be His disciples (see *Matthew 4:21; Luke 5:1-11*).

3. Along with Peter and James, John became one of the three disciples who were closest to Jesus. Most likely he was the one Jesus loved most (see *Matthew 17:1; 26:37; Mark 5:37; 13:3; John 13:23; 19:26; 20:2; 21:7, 20*).

4. John and his brother could at times become too zealous, which may have caused their nickname: "sons of thunder" (see *Matthew 20:20-24; Mark 3:17; 10:35-41; Luke 9:49, 54*).

5. During the events surrounding Jesus' death and resurrection, John stayed as close to Jesus as did any of the apostles. At the cross, Jesus even selected John to take care of His aging mother, Mary (see *John 18:15-16; 19:26-27; 20:2*).

6. Following the resurrection, Jesus revealed Himself to John (see *John 21: 1, 7*).

7. After Jesus returned to heaven, John was often seen together with Peter (see *Acts 3:1; 4:13*).

8. John apparently stayed in Jerusalem for a while and became the leader of the church there (see *Acts 15:6; Galatians 2:9*).

9. We're not sure of much of what went on in John's later years. According to church tradition, at some point he moved to Ephesus, headquarters for seven churches in the Roman province of Asia (see *Revelation 1:11*).

10. John wrote the Fourth Gospel and the letters of *1, 2,* and *3 John*.

NOTES

11. In his later years, John was banished to the island of Patmos, where he received the visions that he compiled as the book of Revelation (see *Revelation 1:9*).

12. It is believed that John died as an old man sometime between AD 95 and 100. His memory has been revered within the church ever since.

The Date and Place for the Writing of the Gospel of John

John probably wrote this Gospel late in his life. There are at least a couple of reasons within the Gospel pointing to that conclusion.

The Gospel doesn't mention the temple in a way to suggest that it was still in existence. So probably the book was written after the destruction of the temple in AD 70. And since the Gospel doesn't refer to the destruction of Jerusalem as if it were fresh news, that event may have already been several years in the past.

The story in *John 21:18-23* suggests that Peter was already dead and that John was an old man who was trying to refute a rumor going around the church that he would never die.

Probably John wrote the Gospel between AD 85 and 95 in Ephesus.

The Purposes of the Gospel of John

1. <u>To establish that Jesus was Divine</u>

    John described Jesus as the Word who became a man (see *John 1:1, 14*). The use of the words "I am" by Jesus reflects the name that God gave to Moses (see *Exodus 3:14*).

    ### *The "I Am" Sayings in the Gospel of John*

Saying	Reference
I am the bread of life	*John 6:35*
I am the light of the world	*John 8:12*
I am the gate for the sheep	*John 10:7*
I am the good shepherd	*John 10:11, 14*
I am the resurrection and the life	*John 11:25*
I am the way, the truth, and the life	*John 14:6*
I am the true vine	*John 15:1, 5*
I am a king	*John 18:37*

John calls the miracles of Jesus "signs" because they point to Jesus' divine nature.

NOTES

The Seven Signs in the Gospel of John

Sign	Reference
Turning water into wine	*John 2:1-11*
Healing an official's son	*John 4:43-54*
Healing a man at Bethesda	*John 5:1-15*
Feeding the five thousand	*John 6:1-15, 25-69*
Walking on water	*John 6:16-21*
Restoring sight to a blind man	*John 9:1-41*
Raising Lazarus	*John 11:1-44*

This Gospel emphasizes more than any of the others the close connection between the Father and the Son.

2. To urge readers to trust in Jesus for Eternal Life

The Gospel says, "And truly Jesus did many other signs in the presence of His disciples, which are not written in this book; but these are written that you may believe that Jesus is the Christ, the Son of God, and that believing you may have life in His name" (*John 20:30-31*).

As one New Testament scholar said, "John's Gospel is fundamentally a call to decision. Like the characters in the story-Nicodemus, the Samaritan woman, Peter, and others-each reader encounters the claims of Jesus and must respond with acceptance or rejection."[17]

An Outline of the Gospel of John

1. Jesus, the Word, Is God in Human Form

    A. Without Jesus, nothing in the universe was made (*1:1-14*)

    B. John the Baptist says Jesus is the Messiah (*1:15-34*)

    C. Jesus chooses Andrew, Peter, Philip, and Nathanael as disciples (*1:35-51*)

2. Jesus Begins His Ministry

    A. He changes water into wine at Cana (*2:1-11*)

    B. He clears the temple of money changers (*2:12-25*)

    C. He teaches Nicodemus that all must be born again (*3:1-21*)

    D. John the Baptist's ministry must become less important as Jesus' ministry becomes more important (*3:22-36*)

NOTES

  E. Jesus tells a Samaritan woman He is living water (*4:1-42*)

  F. Jesus heals an official's son from a distance (*4:43-54*)

 3. <u>Jesus Heals in Jerusalem and Performs Miracles in Galilee</u>

  A. Jesus heals a paralyzed man on the Sabbath (*5:1-15*)

  B. Jesus tells the religious leaders who He is (*5:16-47*)

  C. Jesus feeds five thousand men at the Sea of Galilee (*6:1-15*)

  D. Jesus walks on water (*6:16-24*)

  E. Jesus says He is the bread of life (*6:25-59*)

  F. Some people who were following Jesus leave Him (*6:60-71*)

 4. <u>Jesus Teaches and Heals in Jerusalem</u>

  A. At a festival, Jesus tells people He is living water (*7:1-43*)

  B. Jewish leaders refuse to believe Jesus is the Messiah (*7:44-53*)

  C. Jesus keeps a woman from being stoned for adultery (*7:54¬-8:11*)

  D. Jesus says He is the light of the world (*8:12-30*)

  E. Jesus says that He existed before Abraham (*8:31-59*)

  F. Jesus heals a blind man and accuses the religious leaders of not seeing (*9:1-41*)

  G. Jesus says He is the Good Shepherd, and He and the Father are one (*10:1-40*)

 5. <u>Jesus Raises Lazarus from the Dead</u>

  A. Jesus hears that His friend Lazarus is sick, then hears Lazarus has died (*11:1-16*)

  B. Martha says Jesus is the Messiah (*11:17-37*)

  C. Jesus raises Lazarus from the dead, and the religious leaders decide to kill Him (*11:38-57*)

 6. <u>Jesus Teaches His Disciples during His Last Week</u>

  A. Mary anoints Jesus' feet (*12:1-11*)

B. Jesus rides into Jerusalem in triumph, angering the religious leaders (*12:12-50*)

C. Jesus washes the disciples' feet and predicts Peter will deny Him (*13:1-38*)

D. Jesus teaches He is the only way to the Father, and He is like a vine with us as His branches (*14:1-15:27*)

E. Jesus says the Holy Spirit is coming when He leaves (*16:1-33*)

F. Jesus prays for Himself and His followers (*17:1-26*)

7. <u>Jesus Is Tried, Crucified, and Rises from the Dead</u>

A. Jesus is arrested and tried by the religious leaders as Peter denies Him (*18:1-27*)

B. Jesus is tried before Pilate and sentenced to be crucified (*18:28-19:16*)

C. Jesus is crucified and buried (*19:17-42*)

D. Mary Magdalene finds an empty tomb and meets the risen Jesus (*20:1-18*)

E. Jesus appears to His disciples and convinces Thomas (*20:19-31*)

F. Jesus appears to seven disciples by the Sea of Galilee and forgives Peter for denying Him (*21:1-25*)

Assignment: Read the Gospel of John.

Questions

What similarities do you notice between John and the other three Gospels? What differences?

What parts of the Gospel help you to see Jesus as a member of the eternal Trinity who came to earth for us, and why?

How can the Gospel of John be used in evangelism today?

NOTES

Suggestions on How to Preach through the Gospel of John

"The Word Became Flesh"
Passage: *John 1:1-18*
Key point: Jesus became man so we could become children of God.

"Jesus Explains Being Born Again"
Passage: *John 3:1-21*
Key point: Believe in Jesus and receive eternal life.

"The Woman at the Well Meets Jesus"
Passage: *John 4:1-42*
Key point: Jesus' living water is for anyone who asks.

"Jesus Is the Bread of Life"
Passage: *John 6:25-40*
Key point: We can satisfy our spiritual hunger only with Jesus.

"Jesus Forgives a Sinful Woman"
Passage: *John 8:1-11*
Key point: Forgive others because Jesus forgives you.

"Jesus Heals the Man Born Blind"
Passage: *John 9:1-12, 35-41*
Key point: We all need to see with spiritual eyes.

"Jesus Raises Lazarus from the Dead"
Passage: *John 11:17-48*
Key point: Jesus gives us life that death cannot conquer.

"Jesus Is the Vine and We Are the Branches"
Passage: *John 15:1-17*
Key point: Without Jesus, we can do nothing.

"Jesus Stands Trial before Pilate"
Passage: *John 18:28-40*
Key point: Jesus is the Truth we are searching for.

"Jesus Ends Thomas's Doubting"
Passage: *John 20:24-31*
Key point: We were given God's Word so we can believe.

Chapter Eight
The Words of Jesus

Some Bibles print the words of Jesus with red ink. That way, they stand out from all the other words of the Bible, which are printed in black ink. And that raises a question: are the "red letters"—the words of Jesus—somehow more inspired or more important than the rest of the Bible? And beyond that, what exactly are Jesus' teachings?

Very Important, but Not Exclusively Important

First of all, it's important to realize that the whole Bible is God's Word. As *2 Timothy 3:16-17* says, *"All Scripture is given by inspiration of God, and is profitable for doctrine, for reproof, for correction, for instruction in righteousness, that the man of God may be complete, thoroughly equipped for every good work."* That's **ALL** Scripture. Not just the words of Jesus but also the Bible's law, history, poetry, proverbs, prophecy, letters—everything.

We should also note that the words of Jesus are very important for Christians to know. Jesus ended His Sermon on the Mount this way:

> *Therefore whoever hears these sayings of Mine, and does them, I will liken him to a wise man who built his house on the rock: and the rain descended, the floods came, and the winds blew and beat on that house; and it did not fall, for it was founded on the rock. But everyone who hears these sayings of Mine, and does not do them, will be like a foolish man who built his house on the sand: and the rain descended, the floods came, and the winds blew and beat on that house; and it fell. And great was its fall (Matthew 7:24-27).*

Also, in His Great Commission, Jesus commanded His followers to teach new disciples *"to observe all things that I have commanded you"* (*Matthew 28:20*). To live wisely, follow the words of Jesus. At the same time, remember not to ignore the rest of the Bible.

Creative Teacher

Jesus was called a rabbi, which means "teacher." His closest followers were known as "disciples," meaning students who sat at His feet to learn from Him. And indeed, Jesus was a wonderful teacher.

He taught educated religious leaders, such as Nicodemus. He taught the small group of His disciples. He taught large crowds, such as those who heard the Sermon on the Mount.

He taught formally, as when he preached in synagogues. He taught casually in the midst of everyday life. Sometimes He spoke plainly. Sometimes His words had a mysterious or "hidden" quality. Sometimes He was angry. Sometimes He was sad. Sometimes He was compassionate.

If we want to know Him better (and perhaps preach with His power), we should get to know His Words. We should sit at His feet as His disciples did so often. Below is a chart of some of Jesus' Teachings throughout the Gospels:

Jesus' Teachings

Subject	Reference			
	Matthew	*Mark*	*Luke*	*John*
Beatitudes, prayer, giving, heavenly treasures, etc.	*5-7*		*6:17-49*	
Provision of God, nearness of Christ	*10:1-42*	*6:6-13*		
Sabbath	*12:1-14*	*2:24*	*6:1-11*	
Greatness in heaven, judgment	*11:2-29*		*7:18-35*	
Unforgivable sin	*12:22-45*	*3:19-30*		
Doing God's will	*12:46-50*	*3:31-35*		
Defilement from the heart	*15:1-20*	*7:1-23*		
Humility, stumbling block	*18:1-14*	*9:33-50*		
Hypocrisy	*23:1-39*			
The return of Christ, false prophets	*24:1-51*	*13:1-37*		
Hometown prophet			*4:16-30*	
Christian service			*10:1-24*	
Prayer			*11:1-13*	
God's will, repeat sinners			*11:14-36*	
Purity			*11:37-54*	
Hypocrisy, coveting, blasphemy, watchfulness			*12:1-21*	
Watchfulness, kingdom of God			*12:22-34*	
Born again				*3:1-21*
Worship				*4:1-30*
Doing God's will				*4:31-38*
Eternal life				*5:1-47*
Bread of life				*6:22-71*
Judging				*7:11-40*
Following Christ				*8:12-59*
Christ the door, shepherd				*10:1-21*
Death, eternal life				*12:20-50*
Humility, service				*13:1-20*
Discipleship, Return of Christ				*14-16*

NOTES

Earthly Stories with a Heavenly Meaning

One particular form of Jesus' teaching is especially worth noting: the parable. Jesus told these stories often, using them to teach some lessons in a powerful and memorable way. He said that His use of them fulfilled Isaiah 6:9-10 (see Matthew 13:14-15).

K. R. Snodgrass says, *"Jesus' parables are both works of art and the weapons he used in the conflict with his opponents. They were the teaching method he chose most frequently to explain the kingdom of God… and to show the character of God and the expectations God has for people."*[18]

The Parables of Jesus in the Gospels

Parable	Reference			
	Matthew	*Mark*	*Luke*	*John*
Salt without taste	5:13	9:50	14:34-35	
Christian light	5:14-16	4:21-23	8:16-18	
Wise builder	7:24-27		6:47-49	
Great physician	9:10-13	2:15-17	5:29-32	
Groom's attendants	9:14-15	2:18-20	5:33-35	
New cloth	9:16	2:21	5:36	
New wine	9:17	2:22	5:37-39	
Children in market	11:16-19		7:31-35	
Divided kingdom	12:24-30	3:22-27	11:14-23	
Sign of Jonah	12:38-42		11:29-32	
Unclean spirit	12:43-45		11:24-26	
The sower	13:3-9, 18-23	4:3-20	8:4-15	
Weeds in field	13:24-30, 36-43			
Mustard seed	13:31-32	4:30-32	13:18-19	
Leaven	13:33		13:20-21	
Hidden treasure	13:44			
Householder	13:52			
Pearl of great price	13:45-46			
Net of fish	13:47-50			
Unmerciful servant	18:21-35			
Laborers in vineyard	20:1-16			
Two sons	21:28-32			
Landowner	21:33-46	12:1-12	20:9-18	
Marriage feast	22:1-14			
Budding fig tree	24:32-35	13:28-32	21:29-33	
Wise servant	24:45-51			
Ten virgins	25:1-13			

The Parables of Jesus in the Gospels (continued)

Parable	Reference			
	Matthew	*Mark*	*Luke*	*John*
Ten talents	25:14-30			
Sheep and goats	25:31-46			
Growing seed		4:26-29		
Alert servants		13:33-37		
Two debtors			7:41-43	
Good Samaritan			10:25-37	
Friend at midnight			11:5-13	
Rich fool			12:16-21	
Watching servants			12:35-40	
Wise steward			12:42-48	
Barren fig tree			13:6-9	
Humbled guest			14:7-11	
Feast invitations			14:12-14	
Dinner guests			14:15-24	
Unprepared builder			14:28-30	
King's war plans			14:31-33	
Lost sheep			15:4-7	
Lost coin			15:8-10	
Prodigal son			15:11-32	
Unjust steward			16:1-13	
Rich man and Lazarus			16:19-31	
Servant's duty			17:7-10	
Unjust judge			18:1-8	
Pharisee and tax collector			18:9-14	
Ten minas			19:11-27	
Bread of life				6:31-38
Good shepherd				10:1-18
Vine and branches				15:1-17

Jesus' words are a lasting gift He has given us through the Gospel writers. But it is His life-especially His death and resurrection-that makes our salvation possible. Let us now consider what the Savior has done for us.

Questions

What can you learn from Jesus about being an effective teacher?

Which teachings of Jesus are most important to you? Which ones would you like to understand better?

Which parables of Jesus would you like to retell in your own church planting ministry, and why?

Part 2: The Life and Ministry of Jesus

CHAPTER NINE
AN INTRODUCTION TO THE LIFE OF JESUS

New Testament scholars have long used the term "search for the historical Jesus" to refer to attempts to understand who Jesus really was.

As mentioned in chapter three, some people who have undertaken this search don't believe in the supernatural. They refuse to accept Jesus' miracles, resurrection, and other acts and words that show He is God. What they are left with is a limited and distorted view of Jesus.

But for one who believes in the truthfulness of the Bible, everything we find in Matthew, Mark, Luke, and John adds to the rich resources for our quest to better understand Jesus.

As we have already learned, the four Gospels, though different in some respects, show the same Jesus. His personality and life come shining through clearly in the words of these four books.

The rest of the New Testament fills out our picture of who Jesus is and what He has done for us. And the Holy Spirit in our lives testifies to the truth of the Biblical portrait of Jesus.

Who Jesus Is

Ever since Adam and Eve sinned in the Garden of Eden, the human race has needed a Savior. God gave the Israelites a system of laws and sacrifices, but none of that really saved them. It all just pointed to God's final solution to the sin problem: Jesus.

God sent His own Son—the Second Person of the Trinity—to come to earth as a man. For about three or four years, Jesus carried out a public ministry, teaching people how to know God and demonstrating God's power and love towards them. Dying in our place on the cross, He made it possible for us to be made right with God as we believe in Him. Rising from the dead, He led the way for us to have eternal life.

One scholar states:

> *The thrust of Jesus' teaching was that he brought the promised new era of the rule of God. His mission began with and focused on Israel, but his ultimate goal was to bring the presence and promise of God to the world. The kingdom presence that he began opened the way for the victory of God and the Spirit of God because forgiveness was made possible along with the hope of everlasting life… Jesus portrayed himself as the Son of Man, a human being who possessed divine authority because he also was divine. Jesus according to*

Scripture is far more than a prophet. He is far more than a king who promised deliverance. He is the revealer and explainer of God's plan, as well as the bridge of access to God.[19]

Names and Titles of Jesus in the Gospels

Title	Reference
Jesus	Matthew 1:21
Immanuel	Matthew 1:23
Son of David	Matthew 9:27
Christ	Matthew 16:16
Son of Man	Matthew 20:28
Holy One of God	Mark 1:24
Prophet	Luke 13:33
The Word	John 1:1
Lamb of God	John 1:29
Teacher	John 3:2
Savior	John 4:42
Bread of Life	John 6:35
Light of the World	John 9:5
Good Shepherd	John 10:11
Son of God	John 20:31

He is a miracle worker!

The Miracles of Jesus in the Gospels

Miracles	Reference			
	Matthew	Mark	Luke	John
Healings	4:23-25	1:32-34		
Healing of a leper	8:1-4	1:40-42	5:12-13	
Healing of a centurion's servant	8:5-13		7:1-10	
Healing of Peter's mother-in-law	8:14-15	1:29-31	4:38-39	
Calming of a storm	8:23-27	4:35-41	8:22-25	
Casting out of demons from men at Gadara	8:28-34	5:1-20	8:26-39	
Healing of a lame man	9:1-7	2:1-12	5:18-26	
Healing of a bleeding woman	9:20-22	5:25-34	8:43-48	
Raising of Jairus's daughter	9:18-19, 23-25	5:22-24, 35-42	8:41-42, 49-56	
Restoring of sight to two blind men	9:27-31			

The Miracles of Jesus in the Gospels (continued)

Miracles	Reference			
	Matthew	*Mark*	*Luke*	*John*
Casting out of a demon from a mute man	*9:32-33*			
Healing of a man with a withered hand	*12:10-13*	*3:1-5*	*6:6-10*	
Feeding of five thousand	*14:15-21*	*6:35-44*	*9:12-17*	*6:1-13*
Walking on the water	*14:22-27*	*6:47-51*		*6:16-21*
Healing of a Syrophoenician woman's daughter	*15:21-28*	*7:24-30*		
Feeding of four thousand	*15:32-38*	*8:1-9*		
Healing of an epileptic boy	*17:14-18*	*9:14-29*	*9:37-43*	
Restoring of sight to two blind men at Jericho	*20:30-34*			
Casting out of a demon from a man at Capernaum		*1:23-26*	*4:33-35*	
Healing of a deaf-mute man		*7:31-37*		
Restoring of sight to man at Bethesda		*8:22-26*		
Restoring of sight to Bartimaeus		*10:46-52*	*18:35-43*	
Miraculous catch of fish			*5:4-11*	*21:1-11*
Raising of a widow's son			*7:11-15*	
Healing of a woman with a bent back			*13:11-13*	
Healing of a man with dropsy			*14:1-4*	
Healing of ten lepers			*17:11-19*	
Restoring of Malchus's ear			*22:50-51*	
Turning water into wine				*2:1-11*
Healing of a royal official's son				*4:46-54*
Healing of a lame man at Bethesda				*5:1-9*
Restoring of sight to a man in Jerusalem				*9:1-7*
Raising of Lazarus				*11:38-44*

He is the Messiah!

Prophecies of the Messiah Fulfilled in Jesus

About the Messiah	Prophecy	Fulfillment
Born in Bethlehem	*Micah 5:2*	*Matthew 2:1-6*
His pre-existence	*Micah 5:2*	*John 1:1, 14*
Born of the seed of a woman	*Genesis 3:15*	*Matthew 1:18*

Prophecies of the Messiah Fulfilled in Jesus (continued)

About the Messiah	Prophecy	Fulfillment
Of the seed of Abraham	*Genesis 12:3*	*Matthew 1:1-16*
God would provide Himself a Lamb as an offering	*Genesis 22:8; Isaiah 53:3*	*John 1:29*
From the tribe of Judah	*Genesis 49:10*	*Matthew 1:1-3*
Heir to the throne of David	*Isaiah 9:6-7*	*Matthew 1:1*
Born of a virgin	*Isaiah 7:14*	*Matthew 1:18*
His name called Immanuel, "God with us"	*Isaiah 7:14*	*Matthew 1:23*
Declared to be the Son of God	*Psalm 2:7*	*Matthew 3:17*
His messenger before Him in the spirit of Elijah	*Malachi 4:5-6*	*Luke 1:17*
Preceded by a messenger to prepare His way	*Malachi 3:1*	*Matthew 11:7-11*
Called out of Egypt	*Hosea 11:1*	*Matthew 2:15*
Slaughter of the children	*Jeremiah 31:15*	*Matthew 2:18*
Brought light to Zebulun & Naphtali, Galilee of the Gentiles	*Isaiah 9:1-2*	*Matthew 4:14-16*
Presented with gifts	*Psalm 72:10*	*Matthew 2:1, 11*
Rejected by His own	*Isaiah 53:3*	*Matthew 21:42; Mark 8:31; 12:10; Luke 9:22, 17:25*
He is the stone which the builders rejected which became the headstone	*Psalm 118:22-23; Isaiah 28:16*	*Matthew 21:42; 1 Peter 2:7*
A stone of stumbling to Israel	*Isaiah 8:14-15*	*2 Peter 2:8*
He entered Jerusalem as a king riding on a donkey	*Zechariah 9:9*	*Matthew 21:5*
Betrayed by a friend	*Psalm 41:9*	*John 13:21*
Sold for thirty pieces of silver	*Zechariah 11:12*	*Matthew 26:15; Luke 22:5*
The thirty pieces of silver given for the potter's field	*Zechariah 11:12*	*Matthew 27:9-10*
The thirty pieces of silver thrown in the temple	*Zechariah 11:13*	*Matthew 27:5*
Forsaken by His disciples	*Zechariah 13:7*	*Matthew 26:56*
Accused by false witnesses	*Psalm 35:11*	*Matthew 26:60*
Silent to accusations	*Isaiah 53:7*	*Matthew 27:14*
Heal blind/deaf/lame/dumb	*Isaiah 29:18; 35:5-6*	*Matthew 11:5*
Preached to the poor/brokenhearted/captives	*Isaiah 61:1*	*Matthew 11:5*
Bore our sickness, carried our diseases	*Isaiah 53:4*	*Matthew 8:16-17*

Prophecies of the Messiah Fulfilled in Jesus (continued)

About the Messiah	Prophecy	Fulfillment
Spat upon, smitten, and scourged	*Isaiah 50:6, 53:5*	*Matthew 27:26, 30*
Smitten on the cheek	*Micah 5:1*	*Matthew 27:30*
Given as a new covenant	*Isaiah 42:6; Jeremiah 31:31-34*	*Romans 11:27; Galatians 3:17, 4:24; Hebrews 8:6, 8, 10; 10:16; 12:24; 13:20*
Would not strive or cry, bring justice, have the Spirit on Him	*Isaiah 42:2-3*	*Matthew 12:17-21*
People would hear not and see not	*Isaiah 6:9-10*	*Matthew 13:14-15*
People trust in traditions of men, give God lip service	*Isaiah 29:13*	*Matthew 15:8-9*
God delights in Him	*Isaiah 42:1*	*Matthew 3:17; 17:5*
Wounded for our sins	*Isaiah 53:5*	*John 6:51*
He bore the sins of many	*Isaiah 53:10-12*	*Mark 10:45*
Gentiles gather to Him	*Isaiah 55:5, 60:3, 65:1; Malachi 1:11; 2 Samuel 22:44-45; Psalm 2:7-8*	*Matthew 8:10*
Crucified with criminals	*Isaiah 53:12*	*Matthew 27:35*
His body was pierced	*Zechariah 12:10; Psalm 22:16*	*John 20:25, 27*
Thirsty during execution	*Psalm 22:16*	*John 19:28*
Given vinegar and gall for thirst	*Psalm 69:21*	*Matthew 27:34*
Soldiers gambled for his garment	*Psalm 22:18*	*Matthew 27:35*
People mocked, "He trusted in God, let Him deliver him!"	*Psalm 22:7-8*	*Matthew 27:43*
Cried, "My God, my God why have You forsaken Me?"	*Psalm 22:1*	*Matthew 27:46*
Darkness over the land	*Amos 8:9*	*Matthew 27:45*
No bones broken	*Psalm 34:20, Numbers 9:12*	*John 19:33-36*
Side pierced	*Zechariah 12:10*	*John 19:34*
Buried with the rich	*Isaiah 53:9*	*Matthew 27:57, 60*
Resurrected from the dead	*Psalm 16:10-11; 49:15*	*Mark 16:6*
Priest after the order of Melchizedek	*Psalm 110:4*	*Hebrews 5:5-6; 6:20; 7:15-17*
Ascended to right hand of God	*Psalm 68:18*	*Luke 24:51*

Prophecies of the Messiah Fulfilled in Jesus (continued)

About the Messiah	Prophecy	Fulfillment
Lord said unto Him, "Sit at My right hand, till I make Your enemies Your footstool"	*Psalm 110:1*	*Matthew 22:44; Mark 12:36; 16:19; Luke 20:42-43; Acts 2:34-35; Hebrews 1:13*
He will be a refining fire	*Malachi 3:2-3*	*Luke 3:17*

A Time Line of Jesus' Life

New Testament scholars have tried to come up with dates for key events in Jesus' life but are not in agreement about them.

Most scholars agree that Jesus must have been born no later than 4 BC, because it is well established that Herod the Great died in March of that year. And the Gospels tell us that Herod was alive when Jesus was born.

Luke 3:1-2, refers to the Roman emperor's reign as well as to other rulers in power. This is also helpful in establishing the beginning of John the Baptist's ministry.

But other points are less clear. We know that Jesus was "about thirty" (*Luke 3:23*) when He began His ministry, but how close to thirty? Maybe He was in His late twenties or early thirties. And how long did His ministry last? The estimates range from about one and half years to about four and a half years. We know that He died at Passover, but in what year? Most likely it was no earlier than AD 29 and no later than AD 33.

In short, different scholars come up with different time lines for Jesus' life, and it's not possible to know with certainty which is most correct. This course presents a time line based on the trustworthy work of Johnston Cheney and Stanley Ellisen.[20]

Jesus' Early Years (6 BC - March AD 29)

September 6 BC	Angelic foretelling of John the Baptist's birth
March 5 BC	Angelic foretelling of Jesus' birth
June 5 BC	John the Baptist's birth
December 5 BC	Jesus is born in Bethlehem
February 4 BC	Jesus' presentation at the temple
March 4 BC	Visit of the wise men
Spring 4 BC	Escape to Egypt
2 BC	Return to Nazareth
AD 8	Jesus left behind at the temple
June AD 28	Beginning of John's ministry
January AD 29	Jesus' baptism, temptation
February-April AD 29	Jesus calls His disciples and wedding miracle

NOTES

Jesus' First Year of Public Ministry (March AD 29 – March AD 30)

Spring AD 29	First temple cleansing
December AD 29	John the Baptist imprisoned
January/February AD 30	First rejection at Nazareth
February AD 30	Second calling of disciples
March AD 30	First miraculous catch of fish
March AD 30	Calling of Matthew

Jesus' Second Year of Public Ministry (March AD 30 – March AD 31)

May AD 30	Third calling of disciples
June AD 30	Sermon on the Mount
October AD 30	Calming of the storm
October AD 30	Attending Feast of Tabernacles
March AD 31	Second rejection at Nazareth
March AD 31	Twelve disciples sent out
March AD 31	John the Baptist beheaded
March AD 31	Feeding the five thousand

Jesus' Third Year of Public Ministry (March AD 31 – March AD 32)

April AD 31	Rejection in Galilee
April AD 31	Travels to Gentile areas
April AD 31	Feeding of four thousand
Fall, AD 31	Jesus at Feast of Tabernacles
Fall, AD 31	Conflicts with religious leaders
December, AD 31	Jesus at Feast of Dedication

Jesus' Fourth Year of Public Ministry (March AD 32 – March AD 33)

April or May AD 32	Transfiguration
Summer AD 32	Sending out of the seventy
February AD 33	Raising of Lazarus
March AD 33	Anointed by Mary

Jesus' Final Week and Post-Resurrection Period (March 29 – May 14, AD 33)

Sunday, March 29, AD 33	Triumphal entry
Thursday, April 2, AD 33	Last Supper, agony at Gethsemane
Friday, April 3, AD 33	Crucifixion, death, burial
Sunday, April 5, AD 33	Resurrection

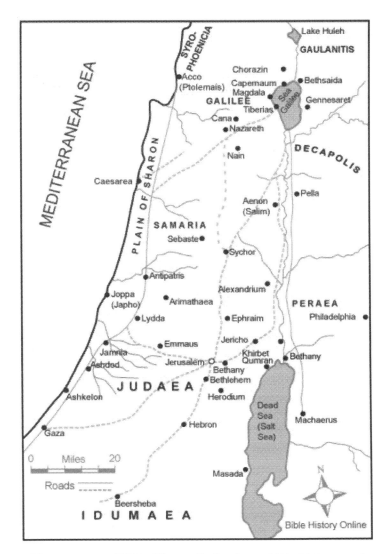

Map courtesy of Bible History Online (www.bible-history.com)

What Jesus' Life Means for All of Us

To quote Darrell Bock again,

> *The question of Jesus is primary because it asks of us not only who Jesus is, but also who we are as God's creatures. If one seeks to know oneself or find life, one must measure oneself against the Creator and his plan. Jesus never is assessed alone, as if his identity were a historical or academic curiosity or merely a matter of private opinion. For what we think of Jesus reveals what we think of ourselves, our capabilities, and our needs, given the way that Jesus presented our need for God and Jesus' own role in that plan…In coming to know him, we will come to know ourselves and our Creator—and in the process find everlasting life.*[21]

NOTES

Questions

Who would you say that Jesus is to you?

Why would you say the people you minister to need to understand that Jesus was a miracle worker? Why do they need to know that Jesus is the promised Messiah?

When you preach Jesus how do these charts help you with your new church?

Chapter Ten
The Messiah's Preparation: Jesus' Early Years

As we have seen, although each of the Gospels has its own characteristics and purposes, they all present a consistent picture of their central figure: Jesus. Thus it is possible to compare the Gospels side by side and try to come up with an accurate story line for Jesus' life on earth.

Books that try to show where the Gospels report the same and different events are called "harmonies" of the Gospels.[22] Christian scholars as early as the second century, including Tatian and Theophilus of Antioch, attempted to produce harmonies. One of the best of modern-day harmonies is called *Jesus Christ: The Greatest Life Ever Lived*, compiled by Johnston M. Cheney and Stanley Ellisen.[23] Indeed, this book is more than just a harmony of the Gospels, since it actually weaves the texts from the four Gospels together as well as tries to put the events on a time line of the life of Jesus.

In much of what follows from here to the end of this book, we are indebted to *Jesus Christ: The Greatest Life Ever Lived*. To see how the parallel passages of the Bible listed below are interwoven, consult that book.

As we consider the life and ministry of Jesus, let us look at each event and teaching in order as they happened (numbered 1 through 208).

The Gospels' Opening Statements

Each of the Gospels has its own way of preparing its readers for the story to come.

1. The Beginning of the Gospel (*Mark 1:1*).
   - The Gospel of Mark begins by identifying its message as the "good news" (Gospel) of Jesus.

2. The Word Made Flesh (*John 1:1-18*).
   - The Gospel of John begins by describing Jesus as the divine "Word," which took on a human body and brought light to the world. This beginning firmly establishes Jesus as divine. Thus a member of the eternal Trinity who was incarnated (became flesh) as a man.

3. The Family Tree of Jesus (*Matthew 1:1-17*).
   - The Gospel of Matthew begins by tracing Jesus' ancestry back through King David to Abraham.

4. Luke's Opening Statement (*Luke 1:1-4*).
   - The Gospel of Luke begins by assuring its original reader (a man named Theophilus) of the care that the author took to report the facts accurately.

Jesus' Birth and Childhood

Jesus' birth, although ordinary in many ways, is also one-of-a-kind. Jesus has Mary for a mother and God for a Father. His birth signals the beginning of a new phase in God's dealings with the human race and is appropriately the subject of angels' songs.

5. An Angel appears to Zechariah (*Luke 1:5-25*).
   - Four approximately hundred years, Israel has received no prophecy from the Lord. But that changes one day in 6 BC when an elderly priest named Zechariah is serving in the temple. An angel appears to him and tells him that he will have a son who will prepare the way for the Messiah. Some months later, Zechariah's wife, Elizabeth, gives birth to John the Baptist.

6. Gabriel appears to Mary (*Luke 1:26-38*).
   - A few months later, the angel Gabriel appears to a young woman named Mary (a relative of Elizabeth's) in the town of Nazareth in Galilee and tells her that she will have a child whom she is to name Jesus. Mary wonders how this could be, since she is a virgin. The angel says that the Holy Spirit will come upon her. This is startling news (a virgin birth of God's own Son!), but Mary humbly submits to this privilege and responsibility.

Hymns of Jesus' Birth in the Gospel of Luke

Traditional Hymn Name	Speaker	Reference
Ave Maria	Elizabeth	*Luke 1:42-45*
Magnificat	Mary	*Luke 1:46-55*
Benedictus	Zechariah	*Luke 1:68-79*
Gloria in Excelsis Deo	Angels	*Luke 2:14*
Nunc Dimittis	Simeon	*Luke 2:29-32*

7. Mary stays with Elizabeth (*Luke 1:39-56*).
   - Mary goes to stay with Elizabeth for a while. The two women sing songs that recognize the wonderful thing God is doing.

8. John the Baptist is born (*Luke 1:57-80*).
   - Elizabeth gives birth to a son, whom Zechariah names John as he was told. Zechariah praises God.

NOTES

9. An angel appears to Joseph (*Matthew 1:18-25*).

   • Mary's fiancé, Joseph, plans to break off the engagement when he finds out that she is pregnant. But then an angel tells him to accept her as his wife.

10. Jesus is born in Bethlehem (*Luke 2:1-21*).

    • Because of a census, Joseph and Mary go from Nazareth to Bethlehem, where Mary gives birth to Jesus in a stable. That night, angels appear to a group of nearby shepherds, telling them that God has done a wonderful thing and urging them to visit the newborn Savior. This they do. The Son of God enters life among humans in a humble way-but heaven has no doubt about His continuing glory.

    • The angel's announcement to shepherds reveals God's ongoing love for simple, humble people everywhere. The Gospel is available to all, including the poor and seemingly ordinary men and women.

11. Simeon and Anna see the Messiah (*Luke 2:22-39*).

    • When Joseph and Mary take Jesus to the temple in Jerusalem some weeks after Jesus' birth, an old man named Simeon and an old woman named Anna recognize Him as the Messiah.

12. Wise men bring gifts to Jesus (*Matthew 2:1-12*).

    • Wise men (probably primitive astronomers) from the East see a star and realize that it means the King of the Jews has been born. They travel first to Jerusalem and then to Bethlehem, where they give Jesus (at this point Jesus is somewhere between the age of a few months old to just under two years) gifts of gold, frankincense, and myrrh.

    • These men represent all the Gentiles who would later give Jesus worship. Jesus is for people of every ethnic group and nation around the world.

13. Jesus' family escapes to Egypt (*Matthew 2:13-23; Luke 2:40*).

    • An angel warns Joseph to take his family to Egypt for safety. Hoping to get rid of Jesus, King Herod kills all boys two years of age and under in Bethlehem. After Herod dies, Jesus' family returns to Nazareth.

14. Jesus stays behind in the temple (*Luke 2:41-52*).

    • When Jesus is twelve, His family takes Him from Nazareth to Jerusalem for one of the important feast days. On their return trip, Mary and Joseph realize that Jesus is not with them. They return to Jerusalem and find Him talking with the teachers in the temple, who are amazed at Him. Jesus' divine wisdom and sense of special connection to the Father are already in evidence.

The Beginning of Jesus' Ministry

NOTES

Throughout His early adulthood (it is presumed), Jesus quietly follows in Joseph's profession as a carpenter in Nazareth. But then, probably in early AD 29, He starts His public ministry. The groundwork for it is laid by John the Baptist, Jesus' cousin and Israel's first prophet in centuries.

15. John the Baptist preaches (*Matthew 3:1-12; Mark 1:2-8; Luke 3:1-18*).

    - John goes to the wilderness at the Jordan River and begins preaching repentance from sin. Crowds come to him, asking questions about the right way to behave. He teaches them, baptizes them, and tells them of the Messiah's coming.

16. John baptizes Jesus (*Matthew 3:13-17; Mark 1:9-11; Luke 3:21-38*).

    - Jesus asks John to baptize Him, and John does. In this way, Jesus identifies with the role of the Messiah. At the conclusion of the baptism, the Holy Spirit descends on Him in the form of a dove and the Father expresses delight in Him—another confirmation of Jesus messianic identity. He carries out His mission in concert with the other members of the Trinity.

17. Satan tempts Jesus (*Matthew 4:1-11; Mark 1:12-13; Luke 4:1-13*).

    - After Jesus' baptism, the Holy Spirit leads Jesus into the wilderness. There Jesus spends forty days without eating. Satan tempts Him repeatedly, but Jesus successfully resists each time.
    - True ministry for God always requires people to resist the temptation to abandon their course.

18. John the Baptist tells who he is and who Jesus is (*John 1:19-34*).

    - Some religious leaders ask John who he is. John identifies himself as one who is preparing for the Messiah. The next day, seeing Jesus, John declares Him to be the Lamb of God.

19. Jesus calls three disciples (*John 1:35-42*).

    - Two of John the Baptist's disciples—John and Andrew—follow Jesus at His request. Andrew talks his brother, Peter, into following Jesus as well. Jesus was beginning the process of putting together a ministry team.

20. Jesus calls two more disciples (*John 1:43-51*).

    - In Galilee, Jesus calls Nathanael and Philip to follow Him. Jesus has begun putting together a team of close followers whom He will use to spread the faith throughout the world.

21. Jesus turns water into wine (*John 2:1-12*).

    - At a wedding in Cana of Galilee, Jesus turns water into wine. This is the first of many miracles to come.

NOTES

Conclusion

Cheney and Ellisen describe this turning point in Jesus' ministry like this:

> *Preparation has been the emphasis in this part of The Greatest Life—the preparation not only of Jesus but also of the message He will present: that He came into the world as the Messiah of Israel, in fulfillment of Old Testament prophecies. The testimonies of Gabriel, Mary, Zechariah, the heavenly host with the shepherds, Joseph, Simeon, Anna, the wise men, John the Baptist, Andrew, Philip, and Nathanael all center on this theme.*
>
> *Now Jesus is about to present Himself to the nation. He will do this at the Passover festival in Jerusalem, Israel's capital.*[24]

Assignment: Choose three of the numbered events or teachings listed in this chapter (1 - 21). Then for each one:

- Read the Gospel passage or passages listed for it.
- State in one sentence the key point you find in it.

Passage(s):
Key point:

Passage(s):
Key point:

Passage(s):
Key point:

Question

How would you preach each of these three events?

CHAPTER ELEVEN
THE BEGINNING OF THE WORK: JESUS' FIRST YEAR OF MINISTRY

With His time of preparation over, Jesus began His first full year of ministry. It likely ran from the spring of AD 29 until the spring of AD 30, and it set the tone for the rest of His public ministry. We see Him participating in a variety of relationships—teaching spiritual inquirers, confronting the sinful, drawing people into the service of God, opposing evil in its many forms.

The first year of ministry is described:

> *The Lord spent much of this year in Judea and by the Jordan River until after John's imprisonment. Back in Galilee, His first general rejection occurred at His home town of Nazareth. From there He went to the region around Capernaum (also in Galilee), where He chose nearly all His disciples. His final choice of Matthew (Levi), a former tax collector for Rome, was a special outrage to Jewish leaders.*
>
> *The shortness of the Gospel writers concerning this first year may appear strange. Matthew, Mark, and Luke pass over most of it, and even John's account seems short. It should be noted, however, that the disciples evidently were not with Jesus during most of this time.*
>
> *Yet it was not a period of inactivity, for Jesus "traveled throughout Galilee" that spring, teaching, preaching, and healing, followed by large numbers of people.*[25]

Jesus in Judea

Jesus probably spends about the first nine months of His public ministry (from the spring till the end of AD 29) in Judea, the southern part of Palestine containing Jerusalem. He is a not widely known at this time, but He is quickly becoming better known, partly because of John the Baptist's testimony about Him.

22. Jesus drives out the money changers (*John 2:13-22*).
    - Attending the Passover celebration in Jerusalem, Jesus gets angry at the people who are turning this house of prayer into a marketplace. So He forces them out of the temple area (This event is distinct from another temple clearing near the end of Jesus' life—*Matthew 21:12*).

23. Jesus talks with Nicodemus (*John 2:23—3:21*).
    - While Jesus is in Jerusalem for the Passover, many people believe in Him. Also, a Jewish religious leader named Nicodemus comes to Jesus one night. Jesus tells him that unless a person is born from above, he

cannot see the kingdom of God. This regeneration (rebirth) is the start of the life of faith.

- Still today, of course, men and women must have a new birth through the Holy Spirit if they are to know God. The message of the Gospel is: you must be born again!

24. John the Baptist praises Jesus (*John 3:22-36*).

- Some of John the Baptist's disciples ask John about Jesus. John plainly states that Jesus is much more important than he is.
- John's humility is a good model for those who represent Jesus. He is the main focus; we are not.

Jesus in Galilee

When John the Baptist is thrown in prison at the end of AD 29, Jesus heads north to His home region of Galilee. There He continues with His ministry and continues assembling His special group of disciples.

25. Jesus speaks with a woman at a well (*Matthew 4:12; Mark 1:14a; Luke 3:19-20; John 4:1-42*).

- John the Baptist is put in prison. This triggers Jesus to head to Galilee. Along the way, He stops in Samaria, a region between Judea and Galilee where people practice a different version of Judaism (Jews and Samaritans are typically unfriendly toward one another). There, even though it is traditional for men not to speak in public to women, Jesus speaks to an outcast woman and leads her to faith in Him.
- In this event Jesus shows us the importance of crossing man-made barriers (ethnic hostility, social customs, and so on) to take the Gospel to those who need it.

26. Jesus heals a royal official's son (*John 4:43-54*).

- A royal official from the town of Capernaum seeks out Jesus in Cana and asks Him to heal his sick son. Jesus does so without even going near the boy.

27. People of Nazareth reject Jesus (*Luke 4:14-30*).

- Preaching at the synagogue in His hometown of Nazareth, Jesus announces that He has personally fulfilled prophecy. At this, the people are convinced that He is guilty of blasphemy and try to throw Him off a cliff. But He walks away safely.

28. Jesus preaches in Capernaum (*Matthew 4:13-17; Mark 1:14b-15; Luke 4:31a*).

- In Capernaum, Jesus calls people to repent and believe the good news; the kingdom of God is coming.

NOTES

29. Jesus calls four fishermen to follow Him (*Matthew 4:18-22; Mark 1:16-20*).
    - At the Sea of Galilee, Jesus calls Peter, Andrew, James, and John to follow Him. Immediately, they go with Him.
    - This story is why evangelists are still called "fishers of men." Anybody who shares the Gospel helps in netting unbelievers and taking them out of the world and into the kingdom of God.

30. Jesus casts out a demon in Capernaum (*Mark 1:21, 23-28; Luke 4:31b, 33-37*).
    - When a demon torments a man attending a service at the Capernaum synagogue, Jesus casts out the demon. This event increases Jesus' fame in the area.

31. Jesus heals many and casts out demons (*Matthew 4:23; 8:14-17; Mark 1:29-39; Luke 4:38-44*).
    - Jesus heals Peter's sick mother-in-law. Then, as He continues to travel about the area, He preaches, heals many, and casts out demons.

32. Jesus helps Peter catch fish (*Luke 5:1-11*).
    - Jesus gets aboard Peter's fishing boat and helps him to pull in a miraculous catch of fish. He tells Peter that the disciple will from then on "fish" for people. That is, Peter will evangelize.

33. Jesus heals a leper (*Matthew 8:2-4; Mark 1:40-45; Luke 5:12-16*).
    - Jesus heals a man's leprosy, then warns him not to tell others about it. But this man disobeys, causing Jesus' fame to spread further.

34. Jesus forgives and heals a paralyzed man (*Matthew 9:2-8; Mark 2:1-12; Luke 5:17-26*).
    - When Jesus is teaching in a crowded house in Capernaum, four men lower their paralyzed friend through the roof. Jesus forgives the man's sins and enables him to walk.

35. Jesus calls a tax collector to follow Him (*Matthew 9:9-17; Mark 2:13-22; Luke 5:27-39*).
    - Jesus calls a man named Levi (or Matthew) to follow Him. This man is a tax collector—a member of a despised profession. Then Jesus attends dinner at Matthew's house, using the occasion to challenge the narrow thinking of the religious people.
    - In Matthew, Jesus found an unlikely partner in ministry. And still today, He calls people of all kinds of backgrounds to serve God alongside Him.

Conclusion

By the end of Jesus' first year of public ministry, there must have been a feeling in Galilee, if not in all of Palestine that something big was happening. Word must have been spreading widely that a miracle worker had appeared. He had amazing things to say about God as well. Who was this man? What was He going to do for the nation? With such a beginning, Jesus' ministry was about to enter its period of greatest popularity.

Assignment: Choose three of the numbered events or teachings listed in this chapter (22 - 35). Then for each one:

- Read the Gospel passage or passages listed for it.
- State in one sentence the key point you find in it.

Passage(s):
Key point:

Passage(s):
Key point:

Passage(s):
Key point:

CHAPTER TWELVE
A TIME OF POPULARITY: JESUS' SECOND YEAR OF MINISTRY

Before we get into the details of Jesus' second year of public ministry, let's consider this overview:

> *Jesus' second year of ministry... was a period of intensive activity and wide public favor. It was also, however, a time of sharp conflict with the religious leaders, causing more of their disapproval. A crucial event that second year was His "Sermon on the Mount."*
>
> *Following that sermon Jesus traveled around Galilee, performing many miracles as a display of His Messianic qualifications. The religious leaders slandered these miracles as Satan-inspired. Responding to this serious charge, Jesus began relying on parables in His teaching. He was turning away from the rejecting nation and instead focusing on receptive individuals.*
>
> *The following spring, John the Baptist was slain by Herod and his queen, an act that outraged the nation. Shortly afterward, Jesus miraculously fed a crowd of thousands and gained so much approval that the Galileans wanted to make Him king.*
>
> *The genuineness of this praise, however, will soon be tested, and their true interests (primarily material and political rather than spiritual) will be exposed.*[26]

Jesus and the Sabbath

Starting His second year of ministry, Jesus faces challenges from the religious leaders. These leaders think He violates their rules about what can and can't be done on the Sabbath, the weekly Jewish holy day.

36. Jesus responds to a challenge by Pharisees (*Matthew 2:1-8; Mark 2:23-28; Luke 6:1-5*).

    - Some Pharisees accuse Jesus of breaking the Sabbath laws because His disciples were harvesting grain by hand. Jesus responds by saying that the Sabbath was made for mankind, not mankind for the Sabbath.

Jewish Religious and Political Groups Mentioned in the Gospels

Group	Description
Pharisees	A group of influential Jewish religious and political leaders who taught strict observance of the Sabbath rest, purity rituals, tithing, and food restrictions based on the Hebrew Scriptures and on later traditions
Sadducees	An elite group of men who followed the laws of the Hebrew Bible but who rejected newer traditions as well as belief in the resurrection and angels
Teachers of the law (Scribes)	Men whose job was to copy the Scriptures, who became influential as interpreters and teachers of the Law, and who acted as agents of the rulers
High priest, chief priests, priests, and Levites	Members of the tribe of Levi who were responsible for the temple and its sacrifices and who thus were the religious and social leaders of the Jewish people
Elders	The older men of a community who formed the ruling elite and were often members of official councils
Sanhedrin	The supreme court of Israel, made up of seventy-one members
Zealots	One of several different revolutionary groups who opposed the Roman occupation of Israel
Herodians	A group that supported the policies and government of the Herodian family

37. Jesus heals a man's crippled hand (*Matthew 12:9-15a; Mark 3:1-7a; Luke 6:6-11*).

    - Encountering a man with a crippled hand in a synagogue one Sabbath, Jesus challenges some religious leaders' legalism by asking them if it's okay to heal on the Sabbath. (The Pharisees had made up religious laws that went further than God's laws in the Scriptures). When no one responds, He heals the man. This angers the religious leaders.

38. Jesus chooses His twelve disciples (*Matthew 4:24-25; 10:2-4; 12:15b-21; Mark 3:7b-19a; Luke 6:12-19*).

    - Large crowds follow Jesus, and He performs miracles for those who need them. Then Jesus spends all night praying and the next morning names twelve of His followers to be apostles (sent-out ones). He continues healing the sick.

NOTES

The Disciples of Jesus

Matthew 10:2-4	Mark 3:16-19	Luke 6:13-16	Acts 1:13-14, 26
Simon Peter	Simon Peter	Simon Peter	Peter
Andrew	James son of Zebedee	Andrew	John
James son of Zebedee	John	James	James
John	Andrew	John	Andrew
Philip	Philip	Philip	Philip
Thomas	Bartholomew	Bartholomew	Thomas
Bartholomew	Matthew	Matthew	Bartholomew
Matthew	Thomas	Thomas	Matthew
James son of Alphaeus	James son of Alphaeus	James son of Alphaeus	James son of Alphaeus
Thaddeus	Thaddeus	Simon the Zealot	Simon the Zealot
Simon the Zealot	Simon the Zealot	Judas son of James	Judas son of James
Judas Iscariot	Judas Iscariot	Judas Iscariot	Matthias

The Sermon on the Mount

In the summer of AD 30, Jesus delivers His most famous teaching: the Sermon on the Mount. *"This was given not as a way of salvation, but to clarify forever the true nature of righteousness and God's kingdom. Jesus reaffirmed the prophet Micah's emphasis—that God desires justice, kindness, and walking humbly with Him—and He sharply distinguished heart-righteousness from mere ritual. Such a message came like a declaration of war to the Pharisees and religious leaders, rejecting as it did their whole hypocritical system."*[27]

39. Jesus teaches about blessings and woes (*Matthew 5:1-2; Luke 6:20-21, 24-26*).

    - Beginning His Sermon on the Mount with sayings known as the Beatitudes, Jesus says that the poor, hungry, and sad will be blessed, while those who have much will suffer. In other words, those who are spiritually humble and aware of their need before God will experience God's blessing.

40. Jesus teaches more about blessings (*Matthew 5:3-12; Luke 6:22-23*).

    - Continuing His Beatitudes, Jesus says that the needy and righteous can expect blessing. God loves to bless those who humbly turn toward Him.

41. Jesus preaches about righteousness (*Matthew 5:13-20*).

    - Jesus calls His followers the salt of the earth—that is, they are to create thirst for the things of God and be a preserving influence in the world (just as salt helps to preserve the quality of meat). Jesus also calls His followers the light of the world—they are to reflect Jesus' truth in the world. He goes on to say that He does not abolish but fulfills the law and that His followers must be righteous.

The Purposes of Salt and Light

Salt .... Flavors, Creates thirst, Preserves
Light .... Shows brightness, Dispels darkness, Shows good works

42. Jesus speaks of true holiness (*Matthew 5:21-37; Luke 12:58-59*).

    - Offering a series of teachings in the form of "You have heard/But I say to you," Jesus compares true righteousness with the legalistic teaching of the rabbis. (Legalism is burdening people with rules that are not required by God in His Word). Jesus compares anger to murder and compares lust to adultery. He also tells His followers not to make oaths (referring not to solemn, official oaths but to oaths made in common speech).

43. Jesus teaches about love (*Matthew 5:38-48; Luke 6:27-30, 32-36*).

    - Once more using "You have heard/But I say to you," and once more giving His followers a completely new concept, Jesus tells them to love their enemies and do good to those who hurt them. This will earn a reward in heaven.

44. Jesus teaches about avoiding hypocrisy (*Matthew 6:1-18*).

    - Jesus makes a contrast between what He wants from His followers and what the religious hypocrites do. He tells His followers to give money in secret, pray in private, and fast without showing it to others. In the midst of this, He also gives them the Lord's Prayer as a contrast to the meaningless prayers of the religious hypocrites.

45. Jesus warns about greed (*Matthew 6:19-24*).

    - Jesus tells His followers to focus on storing up riches in heaven, not storing up riches on earth. A love of money crowds out a love of God. (Compare *1 Timothy 6:10*, where the love of money is called a root of all kinds of evil).

46. Jesus reassures the worried (*Matthew 6:25-34; Luke 12:22b-31*).

    - Jesus tells His followers not to worry about having food and clothing, since the Father will provide what they need.

47. Jesus speaks about relating to others and to God (*Matthew 7:1-11; Luke 6:37-42*).

    - Jesus tells His followers not to judge others, to be generous to others, and to boldly ask God for what they need.

48. Jesus speaks about true discipleship (*Matthew 7:12-20; Luke 6:31, 43-45*).
    - Jesus tells His followers to treat others as they wish to be treated—a teaching known as the Golden Rule. He also tells them to seek the narrow road to life, as the true way is neither popular nor easy. And then He warns about false prophets.

49. Jesus urges obedience (*Matthew 7:21-29; Mark 1:22; Luke 4:32; 6:46-7:1a*).
    - Ending His Sermon on the Mount, Jesus warns that many who are doing works in His name do not really know Him. He tells a parable about two house builders, one of whom builds on sand and one of whom builds on rock. Only the house built on rock (representing a life built on Jesus' teaching) remains standing after a storm. The people were amazed at the authority with which He preached.

Jesus Continues His Traveling Ministry

Jesus uses Capernaum as His Galilean "headquarters," but He travels widely, teaching and performing miracles.

50. Jesus heals a centurion's slave boy (*Matthew 8:1, 5-13; Luke 7:1b-10*).
    - When Jesus returns to Capernaum, a Roman military officer requests that Jesus heal his sick slave boy. Jesus is impressed by this Gentile's faith (so different from the unbelief He had encountered among the Jews) and grants his request.

51. Jesus raises a dead man to life (*Luke 7:11-17*).
    - In the village of Nain, Jesus encounters a funeral procession for the only son of a widow. Jesus brings the young man back to life.

52. Jesus speaks about Himself and John the Baptist (*Matthew 11:2-19; Luke 7:18-35*).
    - From prison, John the Baptist sends some of His followers to see if Jesus really is the Messiah. Jesus sends a reassuring message back to John. Then he affirms John as the greatest of all prophets. He criticizes the people for not listening more to John.

53. Jesus is anointed (*Luke 7:36-50*).
    - As Jesus is having dinner at the home of a Pharisee, a sinful woman pours expensive perfume over His feet. This angers the Pharisees, because they think Jesus should have nothing to do with a sinful person. So Jesus tells a parable that explains why the woman loves Him so much—because God has forgiven her so much. (This event is not to be confused with a similar anointing by Mary of Bethany in the days leading up to Jesus' death).

54. Jesus teaches about evil (*Matthew 12:22-50; Mark 3:19b-35; Luke 8:1-4a, 19-21*).

  - Jesus defends Himself against the charge of being demonized, saying that a demonized person would not cast out demons, as He does. He also criticizes some religious leaders for demanding that He perform a miracle. He says that those who obey the Word of God are His family.

Parables of the Kingdom

One of the key subjects of Jesus' teaching is the kingdom of God. Often He uses stories to suggest what that kingdom is like.

55. Jesus tells a parable about soils (*Matthew 13:1-9; Mark 4:1-9; Luke 8:4b-8*).

  - Jesus tells a parable about a farmer who sows seed on four kinds of soil (hard, rocky, thorny, good), resulting in different responses from the plants.

56. Jesus interprets His parable (*Matthew 13:10-11, 13-23; Mark 4:10-20; Luke 8:9-15*).

  - The disciples ask Jesus why He teaches in parables, and Jesus says that it is in fulfillment of a prophecy in Isaiah. He goes on to interpret the parable of the four soils: each soil represents a different kind of person receiving the Word of God. This explains the different responses the Gospel receives.
  - Indeed, even today, as the Gospel is spoken, many will have hard hearts and reject it completely. Others will hear it but forget it shortly after. Some will respond but will fall away soon after due to the cares and sorrows of this world. Still, in the end, there will always be some who have fertile hearts, accept Jesus Christ and become fruitful disciples.

57. Jesus tells a parable about wheat and weeds (*Matthew 13:24-30*).

  - Jesus compares the kingdom of heaven with a field where wheat grows with weeds until the harvest. The wheat represents true believers in Christ, while the weeds represent false believers (and perhaps especially false teachers) who act as if they are a part of the body of Christ.

58. Jesus tells parables about hidden things (*Matthew 13:12; Mark 4:21-25; Luke 8:16-18*).

  - Jesus tells parables about a lamp being uncovered and a measure being used for both giving and receiving. Just so, God's Word is for sharing generously with others.

59. Jesus tells parables about the kingdom's growth (*Matthew 13:31-35; Mark 4:26-34; Luke 13:18-21*).

  - Jesus tells a parable about a crop growing on its own, about a mustard seed growing into a large plant, and about yeast spreading through

NOTES

NOTES
dough. Likewise, the kingdom of God has its own power of growth inside it.

60. Jesus tells more parables of the kingdom (*Matthew 13:36-52*).
   - Jesus explains to His disciples the parable of the wheat and the weeds: the good and the wicked live side by side in this world, but they will be separated at the time of God's judgment. Then Jesus goes on to tell new parables of the kingdom: it is like treasure buried in a field, a beautiful pearl, and a net full of good fish and bad fish. The parables of the buried treasure and the pearl speak of the great worth of the kingdom, while the parable of the net repeats the point about the good and the wicked being separated at the judgment.
   - Even today, we should not be surprised when we find false teachers, false prophets, and "wolves" gathered in our churches, for this is how Jesus predicted it would be from the very beginning. We must always be on guard and watch, as church planters are called to protect God's flock from spiritual enemies.

Jesus Performs Mighty Acts

Traveling in both Galilee and Judea, Jesus does amazing things—stopping a storm, healing lameness, multiplying food, walking on water, and more—each individually and all collectively proving He must be God.

61. Jesus calms a storm (*Matthew 8:18, 23-27; Mark 4:35-41; Luke 8:22-25*).
   - Jesus and the disciples are in a boat on the Sea of Galilee when a severe storm comes. Jesus calms the storm, revealing His authority over the forces of nature. He criticizes His disciples for lacking faith.

62. Jesus sends demons into a herd of pigs (*Matthew 8:28-34; Mark 5:1-20; Luke 8:26-39*).
   - In Gerasa, Jesus encounters a man inhabited by many demons. Jesus sends the demons into a herd of pigs, which promptly drown themselves in the lake. Jesus sends the man back to his home to tell people what God has done for him.

63. Jesus performs miracles of healing (*Matthew 9:1, 18-34; Mark 5:21-43; Luke 8:40-56*).
   - Back in Capernaum, Jesus encounters a synagogue official named Jairus who begs Him to heal his sick daughter. On His way to Jairus's home, Jesus encounters a woman who had suffered from bleeding for twelve years, and He heals her. Arriving at Jairus's home, Jesus discovers that the girl had died. But He raises her to life. Then Jesus restores sight to two blind men. And He casts a demon out of a man who hadn't been able to speak.

64. Jesus heals an invalid at the pool of Bethesda (*John 5:1-18*).
    - Going to Jerusalem for the Feast of Tabernacles, Jesus heals a man who hadn't been able to walk for thirty-eight years. This rouses the anger of religious leaders, because Jesus performed the miracle on a Sabbath day.

65. Jesus establishes His authority (*John 5:19-47*).
    - Jesus tells His listeners that the Father has given Him His authority. The Father testifies of Jesus, and Jesus comes in the Father's name.

66. Jesus is rejected in Nazareth (*Matthew 13:53-58; Mark 6:1-6a*).
    - Jesus goes to His hometown of Nazareth, where the people refuse to believe in Him. And because of their unbelief, He performs few miracles there.

67. Jesus sends out the Twelve (*Matthew 9:35-38; 10:1, 5-16, 24-42; 11:1; Mark 6:6b-13; Luke 9:1-6*).
    - Jesus sends His twelve disciples out two by two to preach and heal throughout Galilee. Before they go, however, He gives them detailed instructions about what to take and how to act. They are to expect, but not fear opposition.
    - Jesus' instructions are inspiring today to those who take the Gospel into new areas. Not being greedy, sharing the simple message of salvation, being kind to others and yet not letting oneself get distracted by opponents, being bold, trusting in God—these are all good lessons for church planters in our time.

68. John the Baptist is killed (*Matthew 14:1-13a; Mark 6:14-29; Luke 9:7-9*).
    - Herod's wife, Herodias, uses her daughter Salome to pressure Herod to put the prisoner John the Baptist to death. Herod doesn't want to do this, but he gives in. John is beheaded. Later, Herod begins to wonder if Jesus might be John the Baptist returned from the dead.

Rulers Mentioned in the Gospels

Ruler	Reference
Herod the Great (37–4 BC), governor of Galilee and Judea	*Matthew 2:1*
Augustus (27 BC-AD 14), emperor of Rome	*Luke 2:1*
Herod Archelaus 4 BC-AD 6), tetrarch of Samaria, Judea, and Idumea	*Matthew 2:22*
Herod Antipas (4 BC-AD 39), tetrarch of Galilee and Perea	*Matthew 14:3-11; Mark 6:16-29; 8:15; Luke 3:1; 9:7-9; 13:31-32; 22:37; 23:6-15*
Herod Philip (4 BC-AD 39), tetrarch of Iturea and Trachonitis	*Luke 3:1*

Rulers Mentioned in the Gospels (continued)

Ruler	Reference
Tiberius (AD 14–37), emperor of Rome	*Luke 3:1*
Pontius Pilate (AD 26–36), governor of Judea	*Matthew 27; Mark 15; Luke 3:1; 13:1; 23; John 18:28—19:16, 38*

69. Jesus feeds more than five thousand (*Matthew 14:13b-23a; Mark 6:30-46; Luke 9:10-17; John 6:1-15*).

    - The crowds follow Jesus to a spot near Bethsaida, where Jesus preaches to them. Since they are hungry, Jesus multiplies a boy's lunch to feed five thousand men plus women and children.

70. Peter walks on water (*Matthew 14:23b-36; Mark 6:47-56; John 6:16-21*).

    - The disciples are rowing a boat across the stormy Sea of Galilee when Jesus appears to them, walking on the water. He invites Peter to come out onto the water with Him, and Peter does so for a while—until he starts to doubt. Jesus continues to travel and perform miracles.

Conclusion

What extraordinary things our Lord could do! When God walked among human beings, *of course* He healed, taught and did amazing works!

All this got Jesus much attention. But from early in His ministry, He began receiving challenges from some of the religious leaders, who felt threatened by Him. These challenges would only increase. And combined with a fall in Jesus' popularity among the people, the religious leaders' opposition would lead Him closer to His greatest work of all: His sacrifice on the cross.

Assignment: Choose three of the numbered events or teachings listed in this chapter (36 - 70). Then for each one:

- Read the Gospel passage or passages listed for it.
- State in one sentence the key point you find in it.

Passage(s):
Key point:

Passage(s):
Key point:

Passage(s):
Key point:

Question

Which of these events would you like to preach the most in your new church? Why?

NOTES

CHAPTER THIRTEEN
A TIME OF REJECTION: JESUS' THIRD YEAR OF MINISTRY

During Jesus' third year of ministry—spring of AD 31 till the spring of AD 32—things became more difficult. The religious leaders became more determined to oppose Him. And meanwhile, some of the ordinary people turned against Him as well.

None of this stopped Jesus, though it did lead Him to make some changes in His ministry.

> *As the Gospel of John declared, "He came to His own creation and His own people did not receive Him." Though sent to Israel as God's Messiah, Jesus would not force Himself on anyone. Whenever He is rejected—in Jerusalem, Nazareth, Capernaum and across Galilee—He journeys on, finally reaching out to the Gentile areas of Palestine.*
>
> *Facing such widespread rejection, to whom would He now go? The unfolding events give the answer: the prophesied Messianic kingdom will be denied to that generation of Israel, to be fulfilled in a people more ready for it.*[28]

Jesus Clarifies His Identity in Galilee

Early in the third year of Jesus' ministry, His popularity is greatly reduced. First, He is rejected in His ministry "headquarters" of Capernaum. Then a large delegation from Jerusalem arrives, seeking to weaken His influence. All of this causes the number of His followers to get smaller.

71. Jesus calls Himself "the bread of life" (*John 6:22-40*).

    - When some in the crowds seek miracles from Him, Jesus tells them that instead they should focus on believing in Him. He is the "bread of life" who came from the Father. Physical bread, such as the manna that the Israelites ate in Moses' time (*Exodus 16*), is not as important as the "bread" of God's saving presence in Jesus.

72. Jesus calls His body "true food" and His blood "true drink" (*John 6:41-58*).

    - Continuing to explain His self-identification as the "bread of life," Jesus says that He gives His body to "eat." In other words, His sacrifice of His body on the cross would become the means of spiritual salvation. And that sacrifice is symbolized by the Lord's Supper, in which we eat a symbol of Jesus' body and drink a symbol of His blood. The Lord's Supper proclaims the abiding presence of Christ in us, through the indwelling of God's Spirit.

73. Some followers leave Jesus (*John 6:59-71*).
    - Many of Jesus' followers decide to leave Him because of His "hard" teaching. But His twelve closest disciples stick with Him.

74. Jesus' compares God's commands with human traditions (*Matthew 15:1-20; Mark 7:1-23; John 7:1*).
    - Challenged by some religious leaders for His disciples not cleaning their hands according to tradition, Jesus emphasizes God's commands over human traditions. And He says that it's what comes out of a person that makes him or her unclean.
    - The threat of legalism to distract people from following God joyfully and from the heart is ever present.

Jesus Goes to Gentile Areas, Then Returns

Cheney and Ellisen state, "Here a new chapter opens… in the character of Jesus' labors, a transition from dealing primarily with Israel to His going to various Gentile regions."[29]

75. Jesus casts a demon out of a Syrophoenician woman's daughter (*Matthew 15:21-28; Mark 7:24-30*).
    - Jesus heads north to the area of Tyre and Sidon, where a Gentile woman begs him to send the demon out of her daughter. Recognizing her faith, Jesus does as she asks.

76. Jesus heals a deaf and mute man, among others (*Matthew 15:29-31; Mark 7:31-37*).
    - Moving to the Gentile area of the Decapolis (east of Galilee), Jesus enables a man to hear and speak. Then He goes on to heal many others, leading many Gentiles to praise God.

77. Jesus feeds more than four thousand (*Matthew 15:32-38; Mark 8:1-9a*).
    - Still in the Gentile regions, Jesus miraculously feeds four thousand men plus women and children. This is a Gentile equivalent to the time when he similarly fed a large crowd of Jewish followers.

78. Jesus warns of the "yeast" of the Pharisees and Sadducees (*Matthew 15:39—16:12; Mark 8:9b-21*).
    - Back on the western (Jewish) side of the Sea of Galilee, Jesus encounters religious leaders who demand that He perform a miracle for them. Jesus refuses and leaves. Later, Jesus warns His disciples by referring to the "yeast" of the religious leaders. The religious leaders' worldly methods, false teaching, and emphasis on outward behavior instead of inner transformation are dangerous examples to follow.

79. Jesus restores sight to a man in Bethsaida (*Mark 8:22-26*).
    - In Bethsaida, on the shore of the Sea of Galilee, Jesus uses His spit to give sight to a blind man.

NOTES

NOTES

Map courtesy of Bible History Online (www.bible-history.com)

Jesus in Jerusalem

Teaching in Jerusalem is dangerous for Jesus, since this is the center of the Jewish religious system. But He goes there anyway—because the people must know the truth.

80. Jesus goes to the Feast of Tabernacles (*John 7:2-10*).

    - Jesus refuses to accompany His brothers to the Feast of Tabernacles in Jerusalem. But He does go to the feast in secret.

81. Jesus teaches at the temple (*John 7:11-36*).

    - When Jesus teaches in the temple at the Feast of Tabernacles, people misunderstand His words and wonder who He is. Some think He might be the Messiah. Others want to kill Him.

82. Jesus urges people to trust in Him (*John 7:37-8:1*).

    - On the last day of the Feast, Jesus urges people to put their trust in Him, for then they will have "rivers of living water" flowing from them. The people can't decide what to do about Him. Jesus is at risk of arrest, but He leaves the city safely.

83. Jesus releases an adulterous woman (*John 8:2-11*).
    - Trying to trap Jesus, some religious leaders bring a woman caught in adultery and ask Him what to do with her. Jesus, in turn, forces the religious leaders to think about their own sinfulness. He lets the woman go with a warning.

84. Jesus calls Himself the "light of the world" (*John 8:12-29*).
    - When Jesus says that those who follow Him will have the light of life, religious leaders challenge His authority to make such a claim. But Jesus insists that He is saying what the Father says.
    - Jesus is still the Light of the World, and it is our job to see that the world sees this light.

85. Jesus says that He sets people free (*John 8:30-47*).
    - When Jesus says that following Him leads to freedom, some of the people listening insist that they are already free—because they are Jews. But Jesus says they are following their "father" the devil, not the heavenly Father.

86. Jesus rejects the claim that He is demonized (*John 8:48-59*).
    - When some people suggest that Jesus is demonized, He says that He knows the Father. He even claims to be greater than Abraham. After this, Jesus escapes a stoning.

87. Jesus heals a man born blind (*John 9:1-12*).
    - During His travels, Jesus encounters a man who had been born blind. Jesus gives him sight. The man's friends and neighbors wonder what happened.

88. Religious leaders interview the healed man (*John 9:13-34*).
    - Religious leaders question the man whose sight Jesus had restored. The leaders try to make Jesus look bad, but the healed man courageously defends Jesus.
    - Just as this man was kicked out of his synagogue, so many new believers in Jesus around the world face rejection from their families or communities. This is sad. But like the healed man, they need to see that Jesus is worth all they must suffer for His sake.

89. The healed man believes in Jesus (*John 9:35-41*).
    - Jesus seeks out the healed man and invites him to believe in Him. The man does. But Jesus says that some Pharisees are spiritually blind.

90. Jesus calls Himself the Good Shepherd (*John 10:1-21*).
    - Jesus compares Himself to a shepherd and His followers to sheep who know His voice. He says that He will freely give up His own life.
    - We as church planters have the privilege of gathering Jesus' "sheep" into his "sheep fold."

NOTES

Major Hebrew Feasts

Feast	Time of Year	Reference
Passover (Unleavened Bread)	March–April	*Exodus 12:43-13:10; Matthew 26:17-20*
Pentecost (Firstfruits or Weeks)	May–June	*Deuteronomy 16:9-12; Acts 2:1*
Trumpets Also known as Rosh Hoshanah	September–October	*Numbers 29:1-6*
Day of Atonement Also known as Yom Kippur	September–October	*Leviticus 23:26-32; Hebrews 9:7*
Tabernacles (Booths or Ingathering)	September–October	*Nehemiah 8:13-18; John 7:2*
Dedication (Lights) Also known as Hanukkah	November–December	*John 10:22*
Purim (Lots)	February–March	*Esther 9:18-32*

91. Jesus claims unity with the Father (*John 10:22-42*).

- At the Feast of Dedication in Jerusalem, Jesus declares that He is one with the Father. Some of the people pick up stones to kill Him, but Jesus slips away from them.

Conclusion

Twice Jesus narrowly escaped death in Jerusalem during His third year of ministry. His time had not yet come... but it soon would. And He knew this day was coming soon.

Now Jesus will speak clearly to His disciples about His coming death as a criminal. But at His first specific announcement of it, He will also reveal His plan to build His church. He will little by little disclose that plan, all the while training His group of apostles as the foundation for it.

His final year begins with His face turned to the cross—but even that will not be the climax to The Greatest Life. He will introduce His Church and prepare them for rugged service.[30]

Assignment: Choose three of the numbered events or teachings listed in this chapter (71 - 91). Then for each one:

- Read the Gospel passage or passages listed for it.
- State in one sentence the key point you find in it.

Passage(s):
Key point:

Passage(s):
Key point:

Passage(s):
Key point:

Question

How would you preach the Hebrew Feasts in light of your particular culture?

NOTES

Chapter Fourteen
Heading Toward the Cross: Jesus' Fourth Year of Ministry

Jesus had experienced a peak of popularity, and He had lived through a drop in His popularity. But nothing was going to stop Him from completing the mission given to Him by His Father.

The story of His fourth year of ministry is a story of heading toward Jerusalem and the cross. Over the course of the year, He began preparing His followers for what was to come and began wrapping up His public ministry. Jerusalem was ahead.

> "From that time Jesus began to show to His disciples that He must go to Jerusalem, and suffer many things from the elders and chief priests and scribes, and be killed, and be raised the third day" (*Matthew 16:21*).

> "Now it came to pass, when the time had come for Him to be received up, that He steadfastly set His face to go to Jerusalem" (*Luke 9:51*).

Darrell Bock comments,

> *In the journey, Jesus heads for Jerusalem to meet his death... in a journey of divine fate. The entire time he is instructing his disciples, challenging the crowds, inviting them to follow, and confronting the leadership. He is preparing the disciples for what lies ahead and the ministry they will undertake after he is gone. Jesus is giving the crowds more opportunity to respond. He is showing that the way of the current leadership is not the way of God. In this section we get the clearest glimpse of his teaching during the time when many forces are coming against him. This rising conflict sets up climactic events in Jerusalem, and Jesus can see the end.*[31]

Mountaintop and Valley Experiences

In the Transfiguration, Jesus' heavenly glory shines forth—a sample of what He will be like after returning to heaven. But He's still got work to do, and it's no wonder He is disappointed at the failures of His disciples.

- 92. Peter confesses Jesus as the Messiah (*Matthew 16:13-20; Mark 8:27-30; Luke 9:18-21*).
  - Traveling in the area of Caesarea Philippi, Jesus asks the disciples who they think He is. Simon Peter confesses that He is the Messiah. In turn, Jesus calls this disciple Peter, the Rock. Jesus further promises to build His church—the forces of evil, as much as they try, will never succeed in defeating the plans of the all-powerful Lord! (Compare *Ephesians 2:20-21*, where Paul notes that Jesus is still building the church on the foundation He established through His apostles and prophets in the beginning).

93. Jesus prepares His disciples for the future (*Matthew 16:21-28; Mark 8:31—9:1; Luke 9:22-27*).

- Jesus begins to tell His disciples that He will be killed. He also tells them that anyone who wants to follow Him must carry his or her own cross daily. On the one hand, this means that His followers must be willing to accept the "death" of their old, sinful self. On the other hand, and more literally, it means they must be willing to accept martyrdom for their faith in Jesus, if necessary.

94. Jesus is transfigured (*Matthew 17:1-13; Mark 9:2-13; Luke 9:28-36*).

- Jesus takes Peter, James, and John with Him up a mountain, where He is transformed into a being of light. Moses and Elijah appear with Him. The Father speaks, instructing the disciples to listen to Jesus. On the way down the mountain, Jesus explains to the three disciples something of what had happened.

95. Jesus casts out a demon from a boy (*Matthew 17:14-21; Mark 9:14-29; Luke 9:37-43a*).

- The day after the Transfiguration, Jesus casts a demon out of a boy. The disciples had been unable to cast it out because their faith was too weak.

More Ministry in Galilee

During the spring of AD 32, Jesus apparently stays in Galilee. But He continues to prepare His disciples for His death, which will come a year later.

96. Jesus again prepares His disciples for the future (*Matthew 17:22-23; Mark 9:30-32; Luke 9:43b-45*).

- Jesus continues to teach His disciples that He is going to be killed and then raised to life.

97. Jesus asks a question about taxes (*Matthew 17:24-27; Mark 9:33a*).

- When the time comes for Jesus to pay the half-shekel tax for the temple, Jesus implies that He—as the Son of God—shouldn't have to pay a tax to support the temple where God is worshiped. But in order not to cause offense, He miraculously supplies a coin for the tax.

98. Jesus talks about children (*Matthew 18:1-14; Mark 9:33b-50; Luke 9:46-50*).

- Jesus tells the disciples that to be great means to have childlike humility. He also warns against causing children to sin.
- A desire for fame and high position is never the right attitude for those who want to serve Jesus. Following the greatest Servant-Leader ever, we too are to be servant-leaders.

99. Jesus talks about forgiveness (*Matthew 18:14—19:2; Mark 10:1*).

NOTES

- Jesus gives guidelines for what to do when a fellow believer sins against you. Privately at first, then publicly if necessary, you are to confront him about what he has done, with the goal of restoring the relationship. Jesus also tells a parable about a servant who fails to forgive someone else even though he himself has received forgiveness. This means that Jesus' followers, in light of God's great forgiveness of our sins, are to forgive others' sins against us.

Heading toward Jerusalem

Throughout the summer and fall of AD 32, Jesus travels and teaches. What awaits Him in Jerusalem the next year is on His mind, and it is very serious indeed.

100. Jesus seeks commitment (*Matthew 8:19-22; Luke 9:51-62*).

    - When a Samaritan village rejects Jesus, the disciples James and John want to call down fire from heaven. But Jesus rebukes them. Then three would-be followers approach Jesus, and the Lord challenges their willingness to commit to Him.

101. Jesus sends out seventy-two disciples (*Matthew 11:20-30; Luke 10:1-24*).

    - Earlier, Jesus had sent out His twelve disciples two by two. Now He similarly sends out seventy-two disciples in pairs to go ahead of Him. Before they go, He gives them instructions on what to take and how to act. He also criticizes the towns where He had done most of His work, because they had largely rejected Him. Later, the seventy-two return, reporting great success.
    - What a privilege it is to serve God and see the devil's influence shrink!

102. Jesus tells the parable of the Good Samaritan (*Luke 10:25-37*).

    - A religious leader asks Jesus who his neighbor is. In response, Jesus tells a parable about a Samaritan who surprisingly takes care of an injured Jewish man—that Samaritan is a neighbor. Instead of trying to figure out who is your neighbor, so that we can limit our kindness toward just them, we should focus on being a good neighbor to all, even our enemies.

103. Jesus responds to Martha (*Luke 10:38-42*).

    - When Jesus is visiting in their home, one sister (Martha) gets distracted with details while the other (Mary) sits at Jesus' feet. Jesus says that Mary made the better choice. Devotion to Jesus comes first.

104. Jesus teaches about prayer (*Luke 11:1-13*).

    - Jesus gives His disciples the Lord's Prayer as a model. Then He tells them parables that emphasize persistence and confidence when praying.

105. Jesus teaches about demons (*Matthew 12:43-45; Luke 11:14-28*).

    - When Jesus casts out a demon, some accuse Jesus of being demonized Himself. Jesus says it makes no sense for evil to cast out evil.

106. Jesus offers the "sign of Jonah" (*Matthew 12:39, 41-42; Luke 11:29-36*).
    - Jesus says that His generation will have only the "sign of Jonah," referring to His resurrection after three days. He also says that unhealthy eyes lead to darkness (spiritually speaking).

107. Jesus warns religious leaders of destruction (*Luke 11:37-54*).
    - While eating dinner at a Pharisee's house, Jesus gives reasons why the religious leaders' hypocrisy is leading to their destruction: They follow their religious rules carefully yet have no compassion for the needy and no concern about justice. They are proud and selfish. They put spiritual burdens on other people while hindering them from entering the kingdom of God.

108. Jesus talks about fear (*Luke 12:1-12*).
    - Jesus tells His followers to beware of the religious leaders' hypocrisy. They should fear God, not people.

109. Jesus talks about greed (*Luke 12:13-21*).
    - A man tries to get Jesus to defend his side in a conflict over an inheritance. Jesus, in response, tells a parable about a rich farmer who, just after making plans to become wealthier, dies. Wealth is only for this world, and greed is dangerous.

110. Jesus tells the parable of the servants (*Matthew 24:43-44; Luke 12:22a, 32-40*).
    - Jesus tells His followers to be ready for His return the way servants are ready for a master to return from a journey.

111. Jesus explains the parable of the servants (*Matthew 10:34-36; 24:45-51; Luke 12:41-53*).
    - Jesus explains His parable by talking about rewards and punishments. He says that He has come to bring division, since some in a family will believe in Him and others will not.

112. Jesus talks about the weather and a fig tree (*Luke 12:54-59; 13:1-9*).
    - Jesus compares forecasting the weather to understanding the spiritual importance of the times. He warns that the people of His nation are in danger of God's judgment because so many of them reject Jesus. (In fact, the city of Jerusalem will be destroyed in a war about a generation later).

113. Jesus heals a woman on the Sabbath (*Luke 13:10-17*).
    - When teaching in a synagogue, Jesus encounters a crippled woman and heals her. This leads to a conflict with the ruler of the synagogue over healing on the Sabbath.

NOTES

NOTES

114. Jesus talks about the kingdom and His destination (*Luke 13:18-35*).

    - Jesus compares the kingdom of God to a mustard seed that grows and to yeast that spreads through flour. He says that many will seek access to the kingdom and at that time He will say that He doesn't know them. He says that He must keep moving toward Jerusalem to die.
    - Because of Jesus, we are seeing the kingdom of God advance in extraordinary ways in our day.

115. Jesus has dinner at a Pharisee's house (*Luke 14:1-24*).

    - Jesus heals a man with dropsy while at a Pharisee's home for Sabbath dinner. While there, He tells the people to take the lower seats at a dinner out of humility. He also tells His host that, when he is holding a banquet, he should invite the poor and needy. And He tells a parable about a man who did just that.

116. Jesus talks of counting the cost (*Luke 14:25-35*).

    - Jesus urges His followers to count the cost of being His disciple. They must carry their own cross—be willing to give up everything in this life for Him.

117. Jesus talks about a lost sheep and a lost coin (*Luke 15:1-10*).

    - Jesus tells a parable about a shepherd who leaves the rest of his herd to find one lost sheep. And He tells another parable about a woman who tries to find a lost coin. These stories reveal the great love of God for sinners.

118. Jesus talks about a lost son (*Luke 15:11-32*).

    - Jesus tells the parable of the prodigal son. In this parable, a father welcomes back a sinful but repentant son. Meanwhile, the other son resents the father's behavior. This parable, again, teaches the love of God for sinners, but it adds a warning about how religious people can resent that love.

119. Jesus talks about using money (*Luke 16:1-13*).

    - Jesus tells a parable about a steward who shrewdly uses his master's money for his own gain. Similarly, Jesus' followers are to use worldly wealth to gain eternal advantage.

120. Jesus warns the rich (*Luke 16:14-31*).

    - Jesus warns about greed and adultery. He tells the story of a rich man and a poor man named Lazarus, in which Lazarus goes to heaven and the rich man goes to hell.

121. Jesus talks about sin, faith, and duty (*Luke 17:1-10*).

    - Jesus tells His followers to forgive those who sin against them. He says that even a little faith will do mighty works. And He says that people can take no pride when they do right—they are just doing their duty toward God.

122. Jesus heals lepers (*Luke 17:11-19*).
    - Jesus heals ten lepers, but only one returns to thank Him.

123. Jesus speaks about His return (*Luke 17:20-37*).
    - Jesus says not to pay attention to false signs of the coming of the kingdom. He says that "the days of the Son of Man" will come suddenly.

124. Jesus talks about persistence in prayer (*Luke 18:1-8*).
    - In a parable, Jesus tells about a woman who has to keep pestering a judge in order to get justice. Unlike that judge, God is eager to give justice, and so we should pray in faith that He will answer righteous prayers.

125. Jesus talks about humility (*Luke 18:9-14*).
    - Jesus tells a parable about a Pharisee who boasts to God and a tax collector who asks God for forgiveness. It is the humble whom God raises up.

126. Jesus teaches about divorce (*Matthew 19:3-12; Mark 10:2-12*).
    - Responding to a question about divorce from some Pharisees, Jesus emphasizes that God's intention for marriage has always been lifelong unity. Only sexual unfaithfulness is a valid reason for divorce. He admits that this is a hard teaching.

127. Jesus welcomes children (*Matthew 19:13-15a; Mark 10:13-16; Luke 18:15-17*).
    - When Jesus' disciples try to keep children from Him, He orders them to let the children come. The kingdom of heaven is for the childlike—that is, those who have humility and a simple trust in Jesus.

Jesus Nearing Jerusalem

By February of AD 33, Jesus is in lower Palestine, not far from Jerusalem. He appears in Bethany and Jericho, among other places. He is awaiting the right time to enter Jerusalem to give up His life.

128. Jesus goes to Lazarus (*John 11:1-16*).
    - Jesus receives news that His friend Lazarus is sick. Jesus decides to go to Lazarus even though Lazarus's home is in Bethany, near Jerusalem where Jesus would be in danger. Jesus knows that Lazarus has died.

129. Jesus raises Lazarus from the dead (*John 11:17-44*).
    - In Bethany, Jesus announces to Martha that He will raise her brother, and Martha believes Him. At Lazarus's tomb, Jesus prays and then calls Lazarus to come out. Lazarus does.

NOTES

130. Jesus' enemies plot His death (*John 11:45-54*).

    • The high priest and other religious leaders begin seriously plotting Jesus' death. Jesus retreats to the desert.

131. Jesus talks with a rich young man (*Matthew 19:15b-26; Mark 10:17-27; Luke 18:18-27*).

    • A rich young man asks Jesus how to receive eternal life. Jesus tells Him to give away all his money and follow Him. The man does not. At this, Jesus tells His disciples that it is hard for the rich to enter the kingdom.

132. Jesus talks about rewards (*Matthew 19:27—20:16; Mark 10:28-31; Luke 18:28-30*).

    • Jesus assures His disciples that they will be rewarded for all they gave up for Him. He also tells a parable about a master who hires workers at different times during the day, then pays them all equally. God is generous with His rewards and gives them as He sees fit.

133. Jesus tells His disciples what to expect (*Matthew 20:17-19; Mark 10:32-34; Luke 18:31-34*).

    • On the way to Jerusalem, Jesus clearly tells His disciples that He will be betrayed, condemned, and crucified and then will rise again.

134. A mother asks Jesus for special privileges (*Matthew 20:20-28; Mark 10:35-45*).

    • The mother of James and John asks Jesus to give her two sons the highest places in His kingdom. In reply, Jesus tells her that the Father makes those decisions. He also says that His followers are to be servants.

135. Jesus restores sight to a man (*Matthew 20:30-34; Luke 18:35-43*).

    • Near Jericho, a blind man asks Jesus to heal him. Jesus does so.

136. Jesus meets with Zacchaeus (*Mark 10:46a; Luke 19:1-10*).

    • In Jericho, a thieving tax collector named Zacchaeus climbs into a tree to see Jesus. Jesus visits with him and leads him to salvation.

    • Even great sinners, whom everyone else has given up on, will sometimes come to Jesus. They need His grace most of all!

137. Jesus talks about serving Him (*Luke 19:11-27*).

    • Jesus tells a parable about a nobleman who asks his servants to invest his money while he is away being crowned king. When the new king returns and learns that one of his servants had been too fearful to invest the money, the king takes it away from him. The point of this is that, between now and the time Jesus returns from heaven, we are to make the most of the resources God gives us to serve Him.

138. Jesus restores sight to another man (*Matthew 20:29-34; Mark 10:46b-52; Luke 18:43; 19:28*).

- Leaving Jericho, Jesus encounters another blind man, named Bartimaeus. Jesus gives him sight.

Conclusion

Cheney and Ellisen look back at Jesus' fourth year of public ministry, a slow but deliberate journey closer to Jerusalem:

> *Begun perhaps nine months earlier, this journey has taken Him on a crisscross pattern across Galilee, Samaria, Perea, and Judea.*
>
> *The "large banquet" refused by those first invited was instead being offered to "the poor, the crippled, the lame, the blind." Yet, Jesus still demanded decisions of the heart. As great crowds continued to follow, He sought to call out counterfeits and uncommitted. The salvation He offered was free but not cheap or easy. People could come only on God's terms. For those who pursued other priorities in life, Jesus offered no hope.*
>
> *Especially on this last trip to Jerusalem, Jesus emphasized sacrifice. As He revealed His coming cross to His disciples, He spoke also of theirs.*[32]

From Jericho, where Jesus healed a blind man and led a tax collector to faith, Jesus will head to the capital, Jerusalem.

> *The scheduled time for His arrival in the city is the Passover. He had attended the first Passover of His ministry there when He first cleared out the temple abusers. But after John's imprisonment and the beginning of Jesus' ministry in Galilee, He apparently missed the next three Passovers in Jerusalem.*
>
> *For this next [Passover], Jesus intends to be present and prominent. The next part of the story describes this final visit to Israel's capital, where the vengeance of the leaders threatens to explode.*[33]

Assignment: Choose three of the numbered events or teachings listed in this chapter (92 - 138). Then for each one:

- Read the Gospel passage or passages listed for it.
- State in one sentence the key point you find in it.

Passage(s):
Key point:

NOTES

Passage(s):
Key point:

Passage(s):
Key point:

Question

Is Jesus doing miracles in your ministry right now?

NOTES

CHAPTER FIFTEEN
THE WORK OF REDEMPTION BEGUN: JESUS' FINAL WEEK

The term "Passion" is used to describe Jesus' sufferings and death. It is no wonder that each of the Gospels devotes more attention to the Passion than to any other part of Jesus' story. Here is where Jesus fulfilled His mission. Here is where He achieved redemption for all who will believe.

The Passion took place within the space of about a week. Ironically, the week that would end with His death began with the loud praise of the Triumphal Entry. We'll be looking at Jesus' final week in this chapter and the next.

A Time Line of Jesus' Final Week

Sunday	Jesus enters Jerusalem in triumph.
Monday	Jesus curses a fig tree and cleanses the temple.
Tuesday	Jesus' authority is questioned and He teaches in the temple.
Wednesday	Jesus' enemies plan a plot against Him.
Thursday	Jesus shares the Last Supper with His disciples and prays at Gethsemane.
Friday	Jesus is betrayed, arrested, tried, crucified, and buried.
Saturday	Jesus' body remains in the tomb.
Sunday	Jesus rises from the dead!

Darrell Bock states,

> *The final week of Jesus' life is crucial to understanding what his ministry involves. The controversies summarize well the decisive conflict, as do the issues of authority that the temple cleansing raises. The leadership becomes convinced that Jesus must be stopped. It is this decisive confrontation that Jesus foresaw as he approached Jerusalem. He had prepared the disciples for what would come, although they did not seem to appreciate what he had told them. It is in the midst of these controversies and Jesus' teaching about what they would bring that some of the most important elements of Jesus' message emerge.*[34]

Coming to Jerusalem

All of Jesus' life has been building up to His great self-sacrifice for sinners. And now, when the Passover season arrives in AD 33, the time has come to get it started. It begins with Jesus heading into Jerusalem as a humble king.

139. Jesus arrives in Bethany (*Matthew 26:6; Mark 14:3a; Luke 22:1; John 11:55-12:2*).

    - With rumors spreading about whether Jesus would come to Jerusalem for the Feast of Unleavened Bread and Passover, Jesus comes to Bethany, a town near Jerusalem. There he stays with his friends Lazarus, Mary, and Martha.

140. Mary anoints Jesus (*Matthew 26:7-13; Mark 14:3b-9; John 12:3-11*).

    - Mary pours expensive perfume over Jesus' feet—an act that Jesus calls an anointing for His burial. Some of the disciples (including Judas Iscariot) are upset by this apparent wastefulness. But Jesus says she anointed His body for burial.

141. Jesus enters Jerusalem (*Matthew 21:1-11; Mark 11:1-11; Luke 19:29-44; John 12:12-19*).

    - Jesus rides into Jerusalem on a donkey, fulfilling *Zechariah 9:9*. Huge crowds welcome Him as their king. The religious leaders try to get Jesus to quiet the people down, but He refuses. The city is in chaos.

Teaching in the Temple

After His triumphal entry on Sunday, Jesus returns to the temple area several times over the next few days. He gives many crucial teachings during this time. Meanwhile, the religious leaders are getting more and more determined to kill Him.

142. Jesus curses a fig tree and cleanses the temple (*Matthew 21:12-19; Mark 11:12-19; Luke 19:45-46*).

    - Returning to Jerusalem on Monday morning, Jesus curses a fig tree and makes it wither. Then, at the temple, He drives out the money changers. This angers the religious leaders, but ordinary people continue to praise Him.

143. Jesus urges faith and forgiveness (*Matthew 21:20-22; Mark 11:20-26*).

    - On the way to Jerusalem on Tuesday, the disciples ask Jesus about the withered fig tree. Jesus tells them that they can do anything with faith, but they must forgive others.

144. Religious leaders question Jesus' authority (*Matthew 21:23-27; Mark 11:27-33; Luke 20:1-8*).

    - In the temple, the religious leaders ask Jesus by what authority He is doing what He is doing. Jesus silences them by in turn asking them whether John's baptism was from heaven or merely human—a question the leaders can't answer as they would wish without upsetting the crowds.

145. Jesus tells a parable about two sons (*Matthew 21:28-32; Mark 12:1a; Luke 19:47-48*).

    - Jesus tells a parable about two sons, one obedient and one disobedient. The religious leaders are like the disobedient son: they appear to obey God, but in reality they don't.

NOTES

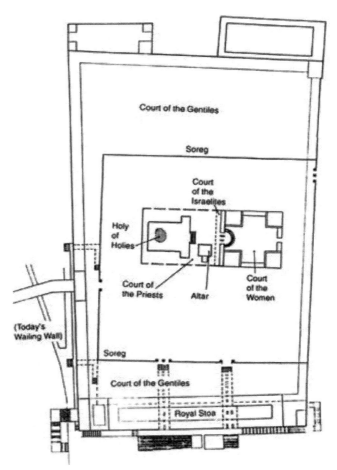

Map courtesy of Bible History Online (www.bible-history.com)

146. Jesus tells a parable about the master of a vineyard (*Matthew 21:33-46; Mark 12:1b-12; Luke 20:9-19*).

    - In this parable, Jesus teaches that God will punish those who kill the prophets and the Son of God.

147. Jesus tells a parable about a wedding banquet (*Matthew 22:1-14*).

    - In this parable, a king punishes someone who attends his son's wedding banquet without an invitation.

148. The religious leaders ask about paying Caesar (*Matthew 22:15-22; Mark 12:13-17; Luke 20:20-26*).

    - Religious leaders, hoping to trap Jesus, ask Him if it is lawful to pay taxes to the Roman emperor. Jesus replies, "Give to Caesar what is Caesar's, and give to God what is God's."

149. Religious leaders ask about marriage in the resurrection (*Matthew 22:23-33; Mark 12:18-27; Luke 20:27-40*).

    - In another attempt to trap Jesus, religious leaders ask about a man who was married seven times—to which woman would he be married in the resurrection? Jesus affirms the resurrection but points out that there is no marriage in heaven.

150. Jesus identifies the greatest commandments (*Matthew 22:34-40; Mark 12:28-34a*).

    - One religious leader (more open to Jesus than the others) asks him a sincere question: which is the greatest commandment? Jesus says the two greatest commandments are to love God and to love one's neighbor.

151. Jesus asks about David's Lord (*Matthew 22:41-46; Mark 12:34b-37; Luke 20:41-44; 21:37*).

    - Jesus asks the religious leaders a question: how can David refer to his own descendant as "Lord"? The religious leaders have no answer. (The answer is that Jesus is the divine descendant of David).

152. Jesus warns about the religious leaders (*Matthew 23:1-39; Mark 12:38-40; Luke 13:34-35; 20:45-47; 21:38*).

    - Boldly, Jesus denounces the religious leaders as hypocrites.
    - Jesus' repeated and angry attacks on hypocrisy should make each of us examine ourselves. Are we emphasizing harmful man-made rules or sticking to the Bible's teaching? Are our hearts filled with pride and self-righteousness or filled with love for both God and people?

153. Jesus praises a widow (*Mark 12:41-44; Luke 21:1-4*).

    - Seeing a poor widow's generosity in giving all she has to the temple treasury, Jesus says that she has given more than anyone else.

154. Jesus says it is time for Him to be glorified (*John 12:20-36a*).

    - When some Gentiles ask to see Jesus, He takes the occasion to teach that He will die and rise again. Any who want to follow Him must follow on that basis.

155. Jesus says He speaks what the Father tells Him to (*John 12:36b-50*).

    - Some believe in Jesus; others don't. Jesus states that believing Him is the same thing as believing in the Father, because He is merely speaking the words the Father gives Him.

Jesus Teaches about the End Times

Jesus' longest teaching during that final week has to do with the end times and His own return.

156. Jesus' warns about interpreting signs of His return (*Matthew 24:1-8; Mark 13:1-8; Luke 21:5-11*).

    - When Jesus predicts that the temple will be destroyed, His disciples ask when these things will happen and what will be the sign that they are to take place. Jesus warns them not to be misled by false messiahs, wars, or natural disasters.

NOTES

157. Jesus warns of persecution (*Matthew 10:17-22; 24:9-10; Mark 13:9, 11-13; Luke 12:11-12; 21:12-19*).

    - Jesus tells the disciples that they will be arrested and mistreated. But this persecution will give them an opportunity to testify of Jesus.

158. Jesus warns of troubles to come (*Matthew 10:23; 24:11-21; Mark 13:10, 14-19; Luke 21:20-24*).

    - Jesus next tells the disciples that war will take place, false prophets will arise, and the "abomination of desolation" predicted by Daniel will appear (*Daniel 9:27; 11:31*). This will be a time of great tribulation.

159. Jesus tells about the Second Coming (*Matthew 24:22-31; Mark 13:20-27; Luke 21:25-27*).

    - Jesus says not to trust false messiahs and false prophets. Signs will appear, and then the Son of Man will appear in glory.

160. Jesus urges the disciples to stay ready (*Matthew 24:32-42; Mark 13:28-37; Luke 21:28-36*).

    - Jesus says that, just as a fig tree's leaves show that summer is coming, so signs will indicate that the kingdom of God is drawing near. No one knows when it will happen, but Jesus' followers should be ready for Him to come and should keep watch.

161. Jesus tells a parable about ten bridesmaids (*Matthew 25:1-13*).

    - Five foolish bridesmaids do not have enough oil for the lamps as they wait for the bridegroom, while five wise bridesmaids made sure to have enough oil. This is a parable about being ready for Jesus' return.

162. Jesus tells a parable about a master who gave his servants money to invest (*Matthew 25:14-30*).

    - A master of an estate gave three servants different amounts of money to invest in his absence. When he returned, he rewarded the two who earned a return on the money, but he punished the one who did nothing. This is a parable about making the most of our time for God while we wait for Christ to return.

163. Jesus tells a parable about sheep and goats (*Matthew 25:31-46*).

    - In this parable the "sheep" (standing for accepted people) receive a king's reward for doing good to the needy, while the "goats" (rejected people) receive punishment for failing to do good to the needy.

164. Jesus' enemies plot against Him (*Matthew 26:1-5, 14-16; Mark 14:1-2, 10-11; Luke 22:2-6*).

    - The religious leaders give Judas Iscariot money to turn Jesus over to them.

A Last Meal Shared Together

Just before He is taken from them, Jesus shares a Passover meal with His disciples. On this occasion, He establishes the Lord's Supper, teaches about love, and prays for the unity of His followers.

165. Jesus arranges a Passover meal (*Matthew 26:17-20; Mark 14:12-17; Luke 22:7-18*).

    - Jesus instructs Peter and John to prepare the Passover meal in a borrowed guest room. Jesus shares this meal with His disciples.

166. Jesus washes the disciples' feet (*John 13:1-20*).

    - Jesus washes the disciples' feet (considered an extremely menial task in that culture) as an example for the way they are to serve others.
    - Humility is always to be the attitude of Jesus' fellow servants.

167. Judas leaves to betray Jesus (*Matthew 26:21-25; Mark 14:18-21; Luke 22:21-23; John 13:21-33*).

    - Jesus says that one of the disciples is planning to betray Him. By giving a piece of bread to Judas Iscariot, Jesus indicates that the betrayer is Judas. The betrayer leaves.

168. Jesus establishes the Lord's Supper (*Matthew 26:26-29; Mark 14:22-25; Luke 22:19-20*).

    - Jesus gives new meaning to the Passover meal He is sharing with His disciples. First, He gives bread to them and says it is His body. Then He gives the cup and says it is His blood. This shows that His death will be the true sacrifice for sin—the reality that the Old Testament sacrifices of animals only symbolized in advance. His death brings about the "new covenant" of a law written on people's hearts and forgiveness of sins (*Jeremiah 31:31-34*).

169. Jesus gives a new commandment (*Luke 22:24-27; John 13:34-35*).

    - Jesus teaches the disciples that greatness comes from serving. He gives them a new commandment: to love each other.

170. Jesus rebukes Peter (*Luke 22:28-34; John 13:36-38*).

    - Peter tells Jesus that he will follow Him. But Jesus predicts instead that Peter will deny Him.

171. Jesus comforts the disciples (*John 14:1-14*).

    - Jesus tells His disciples not to worry. He also assures them that, when they see Him, they see the Father.

172. Jesus asks for obedience (*John 14:15-31*).

    - Jesus tells the disciples that, if they love Him, they should obey His commandments. He also promises to send them peace and the Holy Spirit.

NOTES

173. Jesus calls Himself the true vine (*John 15:1-8*).
    - Borrowing a popular Old Testament image of a vine (*Isaiah 5:1-5*), Jesus tells the disciples that He is the true vine and His Father is the vineyard keeper. They are to abide in Him.

174. Jesus asks for obedience again (*John 15:9-17*).
    - Jesus tells His disciples that, if they keep His commandments, they will continue in His love. They are His friends.

175. Jesus warns of the world's hatred (*John 15:18-25*).
    - Jesus tells the disciples that the world will hate them, just as it hated Him.

176. Jesus promises to send the Holy Spirit (*John 15:26-16:15*).
    - Jesus tells the disciples that, after He dies, He will send the "Helper," the Holy Spirit. The Spirit will convict the world but speak truth to believers.

177. Jesus promises joy (*John 16:16-24*).
    - Jesus reassures the disciples by telling them that though they will grieve for a while, joy will come to them afterward.

178. Jesus promises answered prayer (*John 16:25-28*).
    - Jesus promises that a time is coming when the disciples will ask things in Jesus' name (pray in agreement with God's character and in submission to His will). He is returning to the Father.

179. Jesus says He has overcome the world (*John 16:29-33*).
    - Jesus tells the disciples that, though they will abandon Him, He will not be alone-He has the Father. Jesus has overcome the world.

180. Jesus prays to the Father (*John 17:1-26*).
    - In light of the fact that He is almost done with His mission, Jesus prays that the Father will glorify Him. He also prays that the Father will preserve the disciples and make them holy. And finally He prays for all future believers, that the Father will make them one.
    - <u>All of us were in Jesus' thoughts as He prayed this great prayer</u>! He wants us to be united in the Lord so that the world will see the love of Jesus reflected in us. Jesus prayed for you during this time.

181. Jesus and the disciples go to Gethsemane (*Matthew 26:30-35; Mark 14:26-31; Luke 22:35-39; John 18:1a*).
    - After singing a hymn, Jesus leaves with His disciples for the Garden of Gethsemane on the Mount of Olives. Along the way there, He tells them that they will all fall away from Him. Specifically, He tells Peter that he will deny Him.

Conclusion

Johnston Cheney and Stanley Ellisen say,

> *This part of The Greatest Life closes with the second distinct warning to Peter about his denials of Jesus. These two different warnings (from different Gospels) provide a striking example of the unity and authenticity of the whole account. Far from being contradictory, they describe precisely what will soon take place.*
>
> *Having set His face to the cross and prepared His men for the coming problems, Jesus dismissed Judas the traitor. Now He will fulfill the Father's will in redemptive sacrifice and a powerful resurrection. In these last moments before it all takes place, Jesus will have a final word with the Father, committing Himself fully to His purpose.*[35]

Assignment: Choose three of the numbered events or teachings listed in this chapter (139 - 181). Then for each one:

- Read the Gospel passage or passages listed for it.
- State in one sentence the key point you find in it.

Passage(s):
Key point:

Passage(s):
Key point:

Passage(s):
Key point:

NOTES

Chapter Sixteen
The Work of Redemption Completed: Jesus' Death and Resurrection

Commenting on this final period of Jesus' life on earth, Cheney and Ellisen say,

We have reached the summit of the Life and the turning point of history. Many Old Testament prophecies find their direct fulfillment here, beginning with the first prophecy in Genesis 3:15—that the serpent's offspring would strike the heel of the woman's offspring. But the cross also begins fulfilling the other part of that prophecy—that the serpent's head would be crushed. The final crushing of Satan will include the destruction of his kingdom of darkness and the establishment on earth of God's kingdom of righteousness. All prophecy revolves around these two foretellings of the cross, where Christ fulfilled His twofold commission from the Father: <u>to provide a way of redemption for mankind and to reclaim God's kingdom and authority in all spheres</u>.

In our present age, Christ is fulfilling His redemptive mission. He offers deliverance from sin and death to all who by faith receive Him as their personal Savior. Entering God's kingdom comes only by spiritual birth, a work of the Holy Spirit as one receives this gift of God's Son.[36]

Arrested, Tried, Condemned

Early in the morning of Friday, April 3, AD 33, Jesus is arrested. This begins a series of trials before both Jewish and Roman officials. It all ends with the greatest act of injustice ever—<u>The Son of God is condemned to death</u>.

182. Jesus prays in the garden (*Matthew 26:36-46; Mark 14:32-42; Luke 22:40-46; John 18:1*).

   - Jesus goes with His disciples to the Garden of Gethsemane. While He prays in agony that the cup of suffering might be taken from Him, His disciples sleep. Jesus submits His will to the Father.

183. Jesus is arrested (*Matthew 26:47-56; Mark 14:43-52; Luke 22:47-53; John 18:2-11*).

   - Judas Iscariot arrives in the garden with some soldiers to arrest Jesus. In the conflict, Peter slices the ear off one man, but Jesus restores the ear. Then He leaves with the soldiers.

The Trials of Jesus

Trial	Reference			
	Matthew	*Mark*	*Luke*	*John*
Before Annas (former high priest)				18:12-14, 19-23
Before Caiaphas (current high priest)	26:57, 59-68	14:53, 55-65	22:54, 63-65	18:24
Before the Sanhedrin (Jewish supreme court)	27:1	15:1	22:66-71	
Before Pilate (Roman governor)	27:2, 11-14	15:1b-5	23:1-5	18:28-38
Before Herod (governor of Galilee)			23:6-12	
Before Pilate	27:15-41	15:6-20	23:13-25	18:39-19:16

184. Jesus is questioned by Annas (*Matthew 26:57; Mark 14:53; Luke 22:54a; John 18:12-14, 19-24*).

    - Jesus is taken to the home of the former high priest Annas, who questions Him. One of the officers strikes Jesus.

185. Peter denies Jesus (Matthew 26:58; *Mark 14:54; Luke 22:54b-55; John 18:15-18, 25*).

    - Peter and John follow Jesus to the courtyard of the high priest. Servants ask if Peter is Jesus' disciple, and Peter denies it.

186. The religious leaders condemn Jesus (*Matthew 26:59-68; Mark 14:55-65; Luke 22:63-65*).

    - Jesus is questioned by the religious leadership, who bring in false witnesses to testify against Him. When Jesus admits to being the Son of Man, they condemn Him, then insult and mistreat Him.

187. Peter again denies Jesus (*Matthew 26:69-75; Mark 14:66-72; Luke 22:56-62; John 18:26-27*).

    - Servants at the house of the high priest continue to question Peter of whether he is Jesus' disciple, and Peter continues to deny it. When a rooster crows, Peter remembers Jesus' prediction and begins to weep.

188. The religious leaders confirm their earlier verdict (*Matthew 27:1-2; Mark 15:1; Luke 22:66-23:1*).

    - In a dawn meeting, the religious leaders again gather to question Jesus. Because He admits to being the Son of Man and the Son of God, they think He is guilty of blasphemy and take Him to the Roman governor.

NOTES

189. Judas kills himself (*Matthew 27:3-10*).
- Feeling guilty about what he had done, Judas tries to return the money he had been paid to betray Jesus. Then he hangs himself.

190. Pilate questions Jesus (*Matthew 27:11-14; Mark 15:2-5; Luke 23:2-3; John 18:28-38a*).
- The religious leaders take Jesus before the Roman governor, Pontius Pilate, hoping to get Him sentenced to death. They accuse Him of claiming to be a king. In answer to Pilate, Jesus admits to being a King—but a King whose kingdom is not of this world.

191. Herod questions Jesus (*Luke 23:4-12; John 18:38b*).
- Pilate sends Jesus to Herod, the ruler of Jesus' home district of Galilee. Herod asks Him questions, but Jesus refuses to answer. Herod mocks Jesus.

192. Pilate decides to punish Jesus (*Matthew 27:15-23a; Mark 15:6-14; Luke 23:13-22; John 18:39-40*).
- Pilate tries to release Jesus according to a custom of the Passover. But the crowd won't hear of it; they insist that Pilate release another prisoner, Barabbas. Still trying to avoid crucifying Jesus, Pilate says that He will have Jesus punished and then released.

193. Pilate sentences Jesus to die (*Matthew 27:23b-31; Mark 15:15-20; Luke 23:23-25; John 19:1-16*).
- Pilate has Jesus flogged and beaten. When the people still insist that he crucify Jesus, Pilate questions Jesus again. Finally he gives in to the crowd and orders that Jesus be crucified. The soldiers mock Jesus and then take Him away to be crucified.

Savior on a Cross

At 9:00 A.M. on Friday, Jesus is nailed to the cross. He spends hours suffering from the pain of His wounds, losing blood, struggling to get breath, growing thirsty, and bearing with the mockery of onlookers. That afternoon, He dies. He is buried before sunset.

194. Jesus is crucified (*Matthew 27:32-38; Mark 15:21-28; Luke 23:26-34, 38; John 19:17-24*).
- Jesus carries His cross to a place called Golgotha, speaking to some of the women along the way. At Golgotha, He is crucified between two criminals. The sign over His head states that He is the King of the Jews. Soldiers gamble for His clothing.

195. Jesus hangs on the cross (*Matthew 27:39-44; Mark 15:29-32; Luke 23:35-37, 39-44a; John 19:25-27*).
- Passersby, soldiers, and the crucified criminals mock Jesus. But then one of the criminals asks Jesus to let him into His kingdom, and Jesus says He will. Jesus entrusts His mother into His disciple John's care.

196. Jesus dies (*Matthew 27:45-50; Mark 15:33-37; Luke 23:44b-45a, 46; John 19:28-30*).

    - Jesus cries out to God, and some of the people misinterpret what He is saying. One man gives Him wine so that Jesus might repeat His words. Jesus gives up His spirit to the Father and dies.

Seven Last "Words" of Jesus from the Cross

Statement	Reference
To the Father: "Eli, Eli, lama sabachthani?" "My God, My God, why have You forsaken Me?"	*Matthew 27:46* (see *Psalm 22:1*)
To the Father: "Father, forgive them, for they do not know what they do."	*Luke 23:34*
To the repentant thief: "Assuredly, I say to you, today you will be with Me in Paradise."	*Luke 23:43*
To the Father: "Father, into Your hands I commit My spirit."	*Luke 23:46* (see *Psalm 31:5*)
To Mary: "Woman, behold your son!" To John: "Behold your mother!"	*John 19:26-27*
"I thirst!"	*John 19:28* (see *Psalm 69:21*)
"It is finished!"	*John 19:30*

197. Jesus' death is marked by miracles (*Matthew 27:51-56; Mark 15:38-41; Luke 23:45b, 47-49; John 19:31-37*).

    - At Jesus' death, supernatural signs occur: the curtain in the temple splits in two; an earthquake strikes, opening up tombs from which some of the dead come out alive; and an officer declares that Jesus was righteous. Soldiers pierce Jesus' side with a spear to ensure that He is dead.

198. Jesus is buried (*Matthew 27:57-61; Mark 15:42-47; Luke 23:50-56; John 19:38-42*).

    - A rich man named Joseph asks for and receives permission to bury Jesus' body in his tomb. Joseph and Nicodemus quickly prepare Jesus' body for burial and place it in the tomb.

199. Jesus' tomb is sealed (*Matthew 27:62-66*).

    - To prevent anyone from stealing Jesus' body, the religious leaders ask Pilate to put a guard on the tomb. He agrees.

NOTES

He Is Risen!

On Sunday morning, just as He had predicted, Jesus rises from the dead. Over the next several days, He appears often to His followers, before returning to the Father in heaven.

200. Jesus rises from the dead (*Matthew 28:1-10; Mark 16:1-11; Luke 24:1-12; John 20:1-18*).

- Some women come to Jesus' tomb early on Sunday morning. An earthquake occurs and an angel descends. Mary Magdalene runs to Peter and John to tell them the Lord has risen. The two men go to see for themselves. The risen Jesus speaks to Mary. Other women arrive at the tomb, and the angel speaks to them. Jesus shows Himself to them as well.

201. Soldiers report the resurrection (*Matthew 28:11-15*).

- Soldiers report to the religious leaders what happened at Jesus' tomb. The religious leaders bribe them to lie about it.

202. Jesus speaks with two disciples (*Mark 16:12-13; Luke 24:13-35*).

- Jesus appears to two disciples on the road to Emmaus and teaches them about Himself. The two disciples don't recognize Jesus until they are eating together. The disciples hurry back to Jerusalem.

203. Jesus appears in a locked room (*Luke 24:36-43; John 20:19-23*).

- On Sunday evening, Jesus appears to the disciples in a locked room. He shows them His wounds and eats with them. Then He tells them to receive the Holy Spirit.

204. Jesus appears to Thomas (*John 20:24-29*).

- Eight days later, Jesus appears to Thomas, who had not seen His resurrected body before and did not believe He was alive. Seeing Jesus now, Thomas believes.

205. Jesus appears on the shore (*John 21:1-24*).

- Peter and some of the other disciples are fishing on the Sea of Galilee. Jesus appears on shore and instructs them to cast their net differently, leading to a huge catch. Jesus eats with the disciples. He tells Peter to "feed" His "lambs"—that is, take care of His followers. They discuss John's fate.

- Jesus' words to Peter are His message to all pastors: Feed My lambs. Pastors are to faithfully care for those who follow Jesus under their ministry.

206. Jesus gives the Great Commission (*Matthew 28:16-20; Mark 16:14-18*).

- Jesus meets with His disciples on a mountain in Galilee and commands them to make disciples in all nations.

- This commission is rightfully called great because it is the defining purpose of the Church. Just as Jesus spoke to the disciples, so He speaks to all of us: *"Go and make disciples of all the nations, baptizing them in the name of the Father and of the Son and of the Holy Spirit, teaching them to observe all things that I have commanded you."*

207. Jesus goes up to heaven (*Mark 16:19-20; Luke 24:44-53*).
    - Jesus summarizes the Gospel for His disciples, and then tells them to wait in Jerusalem for Him to send power. Finally He rises to heaven.

208. John tells the purpose of Jesus' story (*John 20:31-31; 21:25*).
    - The selected stories of Jesus are meant to cause readers to believe that Jesus is the Messiah, the Son of God, and to have eternal life.

Conclusion

One scholar says, "The resurrection… means not only that Jesus is alive and that there is life after death, but also that he is shown to be who he claimed to be, given that God has exalted Jesus into His presence in heaven."[37]

<u>It is this risen and exalted Savior whom the four Gospels are all about. It is He we worship and He we preach to the world</u>.

And even His resurrection and ascension are not the end of the story…

On the Feast of Pentecost, a few days after He went up to heaven, Jesus sent the Holy Spirit to take His place as the companion and guide of believers (see *Acts 1:1-10*).

Jesus reigns this very day in heaven. We look forward to His returning to take His church to be with Him and then coming to reign on earth as the victorious King. He will reign forever (see *1 Thessalonians 4:13-17; Revelation 19:11-14; 22:12*).

God desires for all to know His great love for the human race shown in Jesus and to willingly submit to Jesus in obedience. Both King and Servant, both Son of Man and Son of God, our Lord deserves nothing less.

Assignment: Choose three of the numbered events or teachings listed in this chapter (182 - 208). Then for each one:

- Read the Gospel passage or passages listed for it.
- State in one sentence the key point you find in it.

Passage(s):
Key point:

NOTES

Passage(s):
Key point:

Passage(s):
Key point:

Question

How has your view of Jesus changed as a result of this study?

APPENDIX
OUTLINE FOR STUDYING THE LIFE OF CHRIST

Based on *The Life of Christ: A Suggested Outline for Study and Teaching*
by Johnston Cheney and Stanley Ellisen[38]

Lesson 1 (see chapter 10, pp. 66-68)

1. The beginning of the Gospel (*Mark 1:1*).
2. The Word made flesh (*John 1:1-18*).
3. The family tree of Jesus (*Matthew 1:1-17*).
4. Luke's opening statement (*Luke 1:1-4*).
5. An angel appears to Zechariah (*Luke 1:5-25*).
6. Gabriel appears to Mary (*Luke 1:26-38*).
7. Mary stays with Elizabeth (*Luke 1:39-56*).
8. John the Baptist is born (*Luke 1:57-80*).
9. An angel appears to Joseph (*Matthew 1:18-25*).
10. Jesus is born in Bethlehem (*Luke 2:1-21*).
11. Simeon and Anna see the Messiah (*Luke 2:22-39*).
12. Wise men bring gifts to Jesus (*Matthew 2:1-12*).
13. Jesus' family escapes to Egypt (*Matthew 2:13-23; Luke 2:40*).
14. Jesus stays behind in the temple (*Luke 2:41-52*).

Lesson 2 (see chapter 10, p. 69)

15. John the Baptist preaches (*Matthew 3:1-12; Mark 1:2-8; Luke 3:1-18*).
16. John baptizes Jesus (*Matthew 3:13-17; Mark 1:9-11; Luke 3:21-38*).
17. Satan tempts Jesus (*Matthew 4:1-11; Mark 1:12-13; Luke 4:1-13*).
18. John the Baptist clarifies who he is and Who Jesus is (*John 1:19-34*).
19. Jesus calls three disciples (*John 1:35-42*).
20. Jesus calls two more disciples (*John 1:43-51*).
21. Jesus turns water into wine (*John 2:1-12*).

Lesson 3 (see chapter 11, pp. 72-73)

22. Jesus drives out the money changers (*John 2:13-22*).
23. Jesus talks with Nicodemus (*John 2:23-3:21*).
24. John the Baptist praises Jesus (*John 3:22-36*).
25. Jesus speaks with a woman at a well (*Matthew 4:12; Mark 1:14a; Luke 3:19-20; John 4:1-42*).

Lesson 4 (see chapter 11, p. 73-74)

26. Jesus heals a royal official's son (*John 4:43-54*).
27. People of Nazareth reject Jesus (*Luke 4:14-30*).
28. Jesus preaches in Capernaum (*Matthew 4:13-17; Mark 1:14b-15; Luke 4:31a*).

29. Jesus calls four fishermen to follow Him (*Matthew 4:18-22; Mark 1:16-20*).
30. Jesus casts out a demon in Capernaum (*Mark 1:21, 23-28; Luke 4:31b, 33-37*).
31. Jesus heals many and casts out demons (*Matthew 4:23; 8:14-17; Mark 1:29-39; Luke 4:38-44*).
32. Jesus helps Peter catch fish (*Luke 5:1-11*).
33. Jesus heals a leper (*Matthew 8:2-4; Mark 1:40-45; Luke 5:12-16*).
34. Jesus forgives and heals a paralyzed man (*Matthew 9:2-8; Mark 2:1-12; Luke 5:17-26*).
35. Jesus calls a tax collector to follow Him (*Matthew 9:9-17; Mark 2:13-22; Luke 5:27-39*).

Lesson 5 (see chapter 12, pp. 76-80)

36. Jesus responds to a challenge by the Pharisees (*Matthew 2:1-8; Mark 2:23-28; Luke 6:1-5*).
37. Jesus heals a man's crippled hand (*Matthew 12:9-15a; Mark 3:1-7a; Luke 6:6-11*).
38. Jesus chooses His twelve disciples (*Matthew 4:24-25; 10:2-4; 12:15b-21; Mark 3:7b-19a; Luke 6:12-19*).
39. Jesus teaches about blessings and woes (*Matthew 5:1-2; Luke 6:20-21, 24-26*).
40. Jesus teaches more about blessings (*Matthew 5:3-12; Luke 6:22-23*).
41. Jesus preaches about righteousness (*Matthew 5:13-20*).
42. Jesus speaks of true holiness (*Matthew 5:21-37; Luke 12:58-59*).
43. Jesus teaches about love (*Matthew 5:38-48; Luke 6:27-30, 32-36*).
44. Jesus teaches about avoiding hypocrisy (*Matthew 6:1-18*).
45. Jesus warns about greed (*Matthew 6:19-24*).
46. Jesus reassures the worried (*Matthew 6:25-34; Luke 12:22b-31*).
47. Jesus speaks about relating to others and to God (*Matthew 7:1-11; Luke 6:37-42*).
48. Jesus speaks about true discipleship (*Matthew 7:12-20; Luke 6:31, 43-45*).
49. Jesus urges obedience (*Matthew 7:21-29; Mark 1:22; Luke 4:32; 6:46-7:1a*).

Lesson 6 (see chapter 12, pp. 80-82)

50. Jesus heals a centurion's slave boy (*Matthew 8:1, 5-13; Luke 7:1b-10*).
51. Jesus raises a dead man to life (*Luke 7:11-17*).
52. Jesus speaks about Himself and John the Baptist (*Matthew 11:2-19; Luke 7:18-35*).
53. Jesus is anointed (*Luke 7:36-50*).
54. Jesus teaches about evil (*Matthew 12:22-50; Mark 3:19b-35; Luke 8:1-4a, 19-21*).
55. Jesus tells a parable about soils (*Matthew 13:1-9; Mark 4:1-9; Luke 8:4b-8*).
56. Jesus interprets His parable (*Matthew 13:10-11, 13-23; Mark 4:10-20; Luke 8:9-15*).
57. Jesus tells a parable about wheat and weeds (*Matthew 13:24-30*).
58. Jesus tells parables about hidden things (*Matthew 13:12; Mark 4:21-25; Luke 8:16-18*).
59. Jesus tells parables about the kingdom's growth (*Matthew 13:31-35; Mark 4:26-34; Luke 13:18-21*).
60. Jesus tells more parables of the kingdom (*Matthew 13:36-52*).

NOTES

Lesson 7 (see chapter 12, pp. 82-83)

61. Jesus calms a storm (*Matthew 8:18, 23-27; Mark 4:35-41; Luke 8:22-25*).
62. Jesus sends demons into a herd of pigs (*Matthew 8:28-34; Mark 5:1-20; Luke 8:26-39*).
63. Jesus performs miracles of healing (*Matthew 9:1, 18-34; Mark 5:21-43; Luke 8:40-56*).
64. Jesus heals an invalid at the pool of Bethesda (*John 5:1-18*).
65. Jesus establishes His authority (*John 5:19-47*).
66. Jesus is rejected in Nazareth (*Matthew 13:53-58; Mark 6:1-6a*).

Lesson 8 (see chapter 12, pp. 83-84)

67. Jesus sends out the Twelve (*Matthew 9:35-38; 10:1, 5-16, 24-42; 11:1; Mark 6:6b-13; Luke 9:1-6*).
68. John the Baptist is killed (*Matthew 14:1-13a; Mark 6:14-29; Luke 9:7-9*).
69. Jesus feeds more than five thousand (*Matthew 14:13b-23a; Mark 6:30-46; Luke 9:10-17; John 6:1-15*).
70. Peter walks on water (*Matthew 14:23b-36; Mark 6:47-56; John 6:16-21*).

Lesson 9 (see chapter 13, pp. 86-87)

71. Jesus calls Himself "the bread of life" (*John 6:22-40*).
72. Jesus calls His body "true food" and His blood "true drink" (*John 6:41-58*).
73. Some followers leave Jesus (*John 6:59-71*).
74. Jesus' contrasts God's commands with human traditions (*Matthew 15:1-20; Mark 7:1-23; John 7:1*).
75. Jesus casts a demon out of a Syrophoenician woman's daughter (*Matthew 15:21-28; Mark 7:24-30*).
76. Jesus heals a deaf and mute man, among others (*Matthew 15:29-31; Mark 7:31-37*).
77. Jesus feeds more than four thousand (*Matthew 15:32-38; Mark 8:1-9a*).
78. Jesus warns of the "yeast" of the Pharisees and Sadducees (*Matthew 15:39—16:12; Mark 8:9b-21*).
79. Jesus restores sight to a man in Bethsaida (*Mark 8:22-26*).

Lesson 10 (see chapter 13, pp. 88-90)

80. Jesus goes to the Feast of Tabernacles (*John 7:2-10*).
81. Jesus teaches at the temple (*John 7:11-36*).
82. Jesus urges people to trust in Him (*John 7:37-8:1*).
83. Jesus releases an adulterous woman (*John 8:2-11*).
84. Jesus calls Himself the "light of the world" (*John 8:12-29*).
85. Jesus says that He sets people free (*John 8:30-47*).
86. Jesus rejects the claim that He is demonized (*John 8:48-59*).
87. Jesus heals a man born blind (*John 9:1-12*).
88. Religious leaders interview the healed man (*John 9:13-34*).
89. The healed man believes in Jesus (*John 9:35-41*).
90. Jesus calls Himself the Good Shepherd (*John 10:1-21*).
91. Jesus claims unity with the Father (*John 10:22-42*).

Lesson 11 (see chapter 14, pp. 92-94)

92. Peter confesses Jesus as the Messiah (*Matthew 16:13-20; Mark 8:27-30; Luke 9:18-21*).
93. Jesus prepares His disciples for the future (*Matthew 16:21-28; Mark 8:31-9:1; Luke 9:22-27*).
94. Jesus is transfigured (*Matthew 17:1-13; Mark 9:2-13; Luke 9:28-36*).
95. Jesus casts out a demon from a boy (*Matthew 17:14-21; Mark 9:14-29; Luke 9:37-43a*).
96. Jesus again prepares His disciples for the future (*Matthew 17:22-23; Mark 9:30-32; Luke 9:43b-45*).
97. Jesus asks a question about taxes (*Matthew 17:24-27; Mark 9:33a*).
98. Jesus talks about children (*Matthew 18:1-14; Mark 9:33b-50; Luke 9:46-50*).
99. Jesus talks about forgiveness (*Matthew 18:14-19:2; Mark 10:1*).
100. Jesus seeks commitment (*Matthew 8:19-22; Luke 9:51-62*).

Lesson 12 (see chapter 14, pp. 94-95)

101. Jesus sends out seventy-two disciples (*Matthew 11:20-30; Luke 10:1-24*).
102. Jesus tells the parable of the Good Samaritan (*Luke 10:25-37*).
103. Jesus responds to Martha (*Luke 10:38-42*).
104. Jesus teaches about prayer (*Luke 11:1-13*).
105. Jesus teaches about demons (*Matthew 12:43-45; Luke 11:14-28*).
106. Jesus offers the "sign of Jonah" (*Matthew 12:39, 41-42; Luke 11:29-36*).
107. Jesus warns religious leaders of destruction (*Luke 11:37-54*).
108. Jesus talks about fear (*Luke 12:1-12*).
109. Jesus talks about greed (*Luke 12:13-21*).
110. Jesus tells the parable of the servants (*Matthew 24:43-44; Luke 12:22a, 32-40*).
111. Jesus explains the parable of the servants (*Matthew 10:34-36; 24:45-51; Luke 12:41-53*).

Lesson 13 (see chapter 14, pp. 95-96)

112. Jesus talks about the weather and a fig tree (*Luke 12:54-59; 13:1-9*).
113. Jesus heals a woman on the Sabbath (*Luke 13:10-17*).
114. Jesus talks about the kingdom and His destination (*Luke 13:18-35*).
115. Jesus has dinner at a Pharisee's house (*Luke 14:1-24*).
116. Jesus talks of counting the cost (*Luke 14:25-35*).
117. Jesus talks about a lost sheep and a lost coin (*Luke 15:1-10*).
118. Jesus talks about a lost son (*Luke 15:11-32*).
119. Jesus talks about using money (*Luke 16:1-13*).
120. Jesus warns the rich (*Luke 16:14-31*).

Lesson 14 (see chapter 14, pp. 96-98)

121. Jesus talks about sin, faith, and duty (*Luke 17:1-10*).
122. Jesus heals lepers (*Luke 17:11-19*).
123. Jesus speaks about His return (*Luke 17:20-37*).
124. Jesus talks about persistence in prayer (*Luke 18:1-8*).

NOTES

NOTES

125. Jesus talks about humility (*Luke 18:9-14*).
126. Jesus teaches about divorce (*Matthew 19:3-12; Mark 10:2-12*).
127. Jesus welcomes children (*Matthew 19:13-15a; Mark 10:13-16; Luke 18:15-17*).
128. Jesus goes to Lazarus (*John 11:1-16*).
129. Jesus raises Lazarus from the dead (*John 11:17-44*).
130. Jesus' enemies plot His death (*John 11:45-54*).

Lesson 15 (see chapter 14, pp. 98-99)

131. Jesus talks with a rich young man (*Matthew 19:15b-26; Mark 10:17-27; Luke 18:18-27*).
132. Jesus talks about rewards (*Matthew 19:27-20:16; Mark 10:28-31; Luke 18:28-30*).
133. Jesus tells His disciples what to expect (*Matthew 20:17-19; Mark 10:32-34; Luke 18:31-34*).
134. A mother asks Jesus for special privileges (*Matthew 20:20-28; Mark 10:35-45*).
135. Jesus restores sight to a man (*Matthew 20:30-34; Luke 18:35-43*).
136. Jesus meets with Zacchaeus (*Mark 10:46a; Luke 19:1-10*).
137. Jesus talks about serving Him (*Luke 19:11-27*).
138. Jesus restores sight to another man (*Matthew 20:29-34; Mark 10:46b-52; Luke 18:43; 19:28*).

Lesson 16 (see chapter 15, pp. 103-104)

139. Jesus arrives in Bethany (*Matthew 26:6; Mark 14:3a; Luke 22:1; John 11:55-12:2*).
140. Mary anoints Jesus (*Matthew 26:7-13; Mark 14:3b-9; John 12:3-11*).
141. Jesus enters Jerusalem (*Matthew 21:1-11; Mark 11:1-11; Luke 19:29-44; John 12:12-19*).
142. Jesus curses a fig tree and cleanses the temple (*Matthew 21:12-19; Mark 11:12-19; Luke 19:45-46*).
143. Jesus urges faith and forgiveness (*Matthew 21:20-22; Mark 11:20-26*).
144. Religious leaders question Jesus' authority (*Matthew 21:23-27; Mark 11:27-33; Luke 20:1-8*).
145. Jesus tells a parable about two sons (*Matthew 21:28-32; Mark 12:1a; Luke 19:47-48*).
146. Jesus tells a parable about the master of a vineyard (*Matthew 21:33-46; Mark 12:1b-12; Luke 20:9-19*).
147. Jesus tells a parable about a wedding banquet (*Matthew 22:1-14*).
148. The religious leaders ask about paying Caesar (*Matthew 22:15-22; Mark 12:13-17; Luke 20:20-26*).

Lesson 17 (see chapter 15, pp. 104-106)

149. Religious leaders ask about marriage in the resurrection (*Matthew 22:23-33; Mark 12:18-27; Luke 20:27-40*).
150. Jesus identifies the greatest commandments (*Matthew 22:34-40; Mark 12:28-34a*).
151. Jesus asks about David's Lord (*Matthew 22:41-46; Mark 12:34b-37; Luke 20:41-44; 21:37*).

152. Jesus warns about the religious leaders (*Matthew 23:1-39; Mark 12:38-40; Luke 13:34-35; 20:45-47; 21:38*).
153. Jesus praises a widow (*Mark 12:41-44; Luke 21:1-4*).
154. Jesus says it is time for Him to be glorified (*John 12:20-36a*).
155. Jesus says He speaks what the Father tells Him to (*John 12:36b-50*).
156. Jesus' warns about interpreting signs of His return (*Matthew 24:1-8; Mark 13:1-8; Luke 21:5-11*).
157. Jesus warns of persecution (*Matthew 10:17-22; 24:9-10; Mark 13:9, 11-13; Luke 12:11-12; 21:12-19*).
158. Jesus warns of troubles to come (*Matthew 10:23; 24:11-21; Mark 13:10, 14-19; Luke 21:20-24*).
159. Jesus tells about the Second Coming (*Matthew 24:22-31; Mark 13:20-27; Luke 21:25-27*).
160. Jesus urges the disciples to stay ready (*Matthew 24:32-42; Mark 13:28-37; Luke 21:28-36*).
161. Jesus tells a parable about ten bridesmaids (*Matthew 25:1-13*).
162. Jesus tells a parable about a master who gave his servants money to invest (*Matthew 25:14-30*).
163. Jesus tells a parable about sheep and goats (*Matthew 25:31-46*).
164. Jesus' enemies plot against Him (*Matthew 26:1-5, 14-16; Mark 14:1-2, 10-11; Luke 22:2-6*).

Lesson 18 (see chapter 15, p. 107)

165. Jesus arranges a Passover meal (*Matthew 26:17-20; Mark 14:12-17; Luke 22:7-18*).
166. Jesus washes the disciples' feet (*John 13:1-20*).
167. Judas leaves to betray Jesus (*Matthew 26:21-25; Mark 14:18-21; Luke 22:21-23; John 13:21-33*).
168. Jesus establishes the Lord's Supper (*Matthew 26:26-29; Mark 14:22-25; Luke 22:19-20*).
169. Jesus gives a new commandment (*Luke 22:24-27; John 13:34-35*).
170. Jesus rebukes Peter (*Luke 22:28-34; John 13:36-38*).
171. Jesus comforts the disciples (*John 14:1-14*).
172. Jesus asks for obedience (*John 14:15-31*).

Lesson 19 (see chapter 15, p. 108)

173. Jesus calls Himself the true vine (*John 15:1-8*).
174. Jesus asks for obedience again (*John 15:9-17*).
175. Jesus warns of the world's hatred (*John 15:18-25*).
176. Jesus promises to send the Holy Spirit (*John 15:26-16:15*).
177. Jesus promises joy (*John 16:16-24*).
178. Jesus promises answered prayer (*John 16:25-28*).
179. Jesus says He has overcome the world (*John 16:29-33*).
180. Jesus prays to the Father (*John 17:1-26*).
181. Jesus and the disciples go to Gethsemane (*Matthew 26:30-35; Mark 14:26-31; Luke 22:35-39; John 18:1a*).

NOTES **Lesson 20** (see chapter 16, pp. 110-112)

182. Jesus prays in the garden (*Matthew 26:36-46; Mark 14:32-42; Luke 22:40-46; John 18:1b*).
183. Jesus is arrested (*Matthew 26:47-56; Mark 14:43-52; Luke 22:47-53; John 18:2-11*).
184. Jesus is questioned by Annas (*Matthew 26:57; Mark 14:53; Luke 22:54a; John 18:12-14, 19-24*).
185. Peter denies Jesus (*Matthew 26:58; Mark 14:54; Luke 22:54b-55; John 18:15-18, 25*).
186. The religious leaders condemn Jesus (*Matthew 26:59-68; Mark 14:55-65; Luke 22:63-65*).
187. Peter again denies Jesus (*Matthew 26:69-75; Mark 14:66-72; Luke 22:56-62; John 18:26-27*).
188. The religious leaders confirm their earlier verdict (*Matthew 27:1-2; Mark 15:1; Luke 22:66-23:1*).
189. Judas kills himself (*Matthew 27:3-10*).
190. Pilate questions Jesus (*Matthew 27:11-14; Mark 15:2-5; Luke 23:2-3; John 18:28-38a*).
191. Herod questions Jesus (*Luke 23:4-12; John 18:38b*).

Lesson 21 (see chapter 16, pp. 112-113)

192. Pilate decides to punish Jesus (*Matthew 27:15-23a; Mark 15:6-14; Luke 23:13-22; John 18:39-40*).
193. Pilate sentences Jesus to die (*Matthew 27:23b-31; Mark 15:15-20; Luke 23:23-25; John 19:1-16*).
194. Jesus is crucified (*Matthew 27:32-38; Mark 15:21-28; Luke 23:26-34, 38; John 19:17-24*).
195. Jesus hangs on the cross (*Matthew 27:39-44; Mark 15:29-32; Luke 23:35-37, 39-44a; John 19:25-27*).
196. Jesus dies (*Matthew 27:45-50; Mark 15:33-37; Luke 23:44b-45a, 46; John 19:28-30*).
197. Jesus' death is marked by miracles (*Matthew 27:51-56; Mark 15:38-41; Luke 23:45b, 47-49; John 19:31-37*).
198. Jesus is buried (*Matthew 27:57-61; Mark 15:42-47; Luke 23:50-56; John 19:38-42*).
199. Jesus' tomb is sealed (*Matthew 27:62-66*).

Lesson 22 (see chapter 16, pp. 114-115)

200. Jesus rises from the dead (*Matthew 28:1-10; Mark 16:1-11; Luke 24:1-12; John 20:1-18*).
201. Soldiers report the resurrection (*Matthew 28:11-15*).
202. Jesus speaks with two disciples (*Mark 16:12-13; Luke 24:13-35*).
203. Jesus appears in a locked room (*Luke 24:36-43; John 20:19-23*).
204. Jesus appears to Thomas (*John 20:24-29*).
205. Jesus appears on the shore (*John 21:1-24*).
206. Jesus gives the Great Commission (*Matthew 28:16-20; Mark 16:14-18*).
207. Jesus goes up to heaven (*Mark 16:19-20; Luke 24:44-53*).
208. John tells the purpose of Jesus' story (*John 20:31-31; 21:25*).

ENDNOTES

1. Over the years, the four creatures have been assigned to the Gospels in different orders. The order shown here comes from Norman L. Geisler, *A Popular Survey of the New Testament* (Grand Rapids, MI: Baker, 2007), 47.

2. Craig L. Blomberg, *Jesus and the Gospels: An Introduction and Survey*, 2nd ed. (Nashville: B&H, 2009), 7.

3. Mark L. Strauss, *Four Portraits, One Jesus: An Introduction to Jesus and the Gospels* (Grand Rapids, MI: Zondervan, 2007), 24.

4. Norman L. Geisler, *A Popular Survey of the New Testament* (Grand Rapids, MI: Baker, 2007), 46–47.

5. Strauss, 32.

6. Adapted from ibid., 173, 215, 261, 299.

7. L. W. Hurtado, "Gospel (Genre)," in *Dictionary of Jesus and the Gospels*, ed. Joel B. Green and Scot McKnight (Downers Grove, IL: InterVarsity Press, 1992), 282.

8. I. Howard Marshall, "The Gospels and Jesus Christ," in *Eerdmans Handbook to the Bible*, ed. David Alexander and Pat Alexander (Grand Rapids, MI: Eerdmans, 1992), 470.

9. These are, of course, not the only apparent contradictions in the Gospels. For more help, see Norman L. Geisler, *When Critics Ask: A Popular Handbook on Bible Difficulties* (Grand Rapids, MI: Baker, 1992), 325–436.

10. Mark L. Strauss, *Four Portraits, One Jesus: An Introduction to Jesus and the Gospels* (Grand Rapids, MI: Zondervan, 2007), 253.

11. Mark L. Strauss, *Four Portraits, One Jesus: An Introduction to Jesus and the Gospels* (Grand Rapids, MI: Zondervan, 2007), 205.

12. R. A. Guelich, "Gospel of Mark," in *Dictionary of Jesus and the Gospels*, ed. Joel B. Green and Scot McKnight (Downers Grove, IL: InterVarsity Press, 1992), 524–5.

13. Ray C. Stedman, *The Servant Who Rules* (Waco, TX: Word, 1976); and Ray C. Stedman, *The Ruler Who Serves* (Waco, TX: Word, 1976).

14. F. W. Burnett, "Gospel of Luke," in *Dictionary of Jesus and the Gospels*, ed. Joel B. Green and Scot McKnight (Downers Grove, IL: InterVarsity Press, 1992), 509.

15. Mark L. Strauss, *Four Portraits, One Jesus: An Introduction to Jesus and the Gospels* (Grand Rapids, MI: Zondervan, 2007), 290–91.

16. Of course, John does not ignore Jesus' humanity any more than Luke ignores Jesus' divinity.

17. Mark L. Strauss, *Four Portraits, One Jesus: An Introduction to Jesus and the Gospels* (Grand Rapids, MI: Zondervan, 2007), 337.

18. K. R. Snodgrass, "Parable," in *Dictionary of Jesus and the Gospels*, ed. Joel B. Green and Scot McKnight (Downers Grove, IL: InterVarsity Press, 1992), 591.

19. Darrell L. Bock, *Jesus According to Scripture: Restoring the Portrait from the Gospels* (Grand Rapids, MI: Baker, 2002), 646–7.

20. Johnston M. Cheney and Stanley Ellisen, comp. and trans., *Jesus Christ: The Greatest Life Ever Lived* (Eugene, OR: Paradise, 1999), 26, 48, 66, 110, 138, 269, 271–9.

21. Bock, 647–8.

22. For an example of a "harmony," see J. Dwight Pentecost, *A Harmony of the Words and Works of Jesus Christ* (Grand Rapids, MI: Zondervan, 1981); or Robert L. Thomas and Stanley N. Gundry, *The NIV Harmony of the Gospels* (San Francisco: Harper & Row, 1988).

23. Johnston M. Cheney and Stanley Ellisen, comp. and trans., *Jesus Christ: The Greatest Life Ever Lived* (Eugene, OR: Paradise, 1999). See also the related one-year devotional book: R. A. Meltebeke and Ed Stewart, *Jesus 365: Experiencing the Four Gospels as One Single Story* (Eugene, OR: Harvest House, 2008).

24. Cheney and Ellisen, 46.

25. Johnston M. Cheney and Stanley Ellisen, comp. and trans., *Jesus Christ: The Greatest Life Ever Lived* (Eugene, OR: Paradise, 1999), 64.

26. Johnston M. Cheney and Stanley Ellisen, comp. and trans., *Jesus Christ: The Greatest Life Ever Lived* (Eugene, OR: Paradise, 1999), 108.

27. Ibid.

28. Johnston M. Cheney and Stanley Ellisen, comp. and trans., *Jesus Christ: The Greatest Life Ever Lived* (Eugene, OR: Paradise, 1999), 134.

29. Ibid., 116.

30. Ibid.

31. Darrell L. Bock, *Jesus According to Scripture: Restoring the Portrait from the Gospels* (Grand Rapids, MI: Baker, 2002), 249.

32. Johnston M. Cheney and Stanley Ellisen, comp. and trans., *Jesus Christ: The Greatest Life Ever Lived* (Eugene, OR: Paradise, 1999), 187.

33. Ibid.

34. Darrell L. Bock, *Jesus According to Scripture: Restoring the Portrait from the Gospels* (Grand Rapids, MI: Baker, 2002), 317–8.

35. Johnston M. Cheney and Stanley Ellisen, comp. and trans., *Jesus Christ: The Greatest Life Ever Lived* (Eugene, OR: Paradise, 1999), 233.

36. Johnston M. Cheney and Stanley Ellisen, comp. and trans., *Jesus Christ: The Greatest Life Ever Lived* (Eugene, OR: Paradise, 1999), 267.

37. Darrell L. Bock, *Jesus According to Scripture: Restoring the Portrait from the Gospels* (Grand Rapids, MI: Baker, 2002), 645.

38. Johnston M. Cheney and Stanley Ellisen, comp. and trans., *Jesus Christ: The Greatest Life Ever Lived* (Eugene, OR: Paradise, 1999), 281–5.

Additional Resource Guide

Blomberg, Craig. *Jesus and the Gospels: An Introduction and Survey*, 2nd ed. Nashville: B&H, 2009.

Bock, Darrell L. *Jesus According to Scripture: Restoring the Portrait from the Gospels*. Grand Rapids, MI: Baker, 2002.

Burridge, Richard A. *Four Gospels, One Jesus? A Symbolic Reading*, 2nd ed. Grand Rapids, MI: Eerdmans, 2005.

Cheney, Johnston M., and Stanley Ellisen, comp and trans. *Jesus Christ: The Greatest Life Ever Lived*. Eugene, OR: Paradise, 1999.

Flynn, Leslie B. *Four Faces of Jesus: The Uniqueness of the Gospel Narratives*. Grand Rapids, MI: Kregel, 1993.

Green, Joel B., and Scot McKnight. *Dictionary of Jesus and the Gospels*. Downers Grove, IL: InterVarsity Press, 1992.

Strauss, Mark L. *Four Portraits, One Jesus: An Introduction to Jesus and the Gospels*. Grand Rapids, MI: Zondervan, 2007

Made in the USA
Columbia, SC
26 May 2018